BIG

CAITLIN PRESS INC.
8100 Alderwood Road,
Halfmoon Bay, BC VON 1Y1
www.caitlin-press.com

Text design by Shed Simas / Onça Design
Cover design by Monica Miller
Cover image from iStock ID 1091423892
Printed in Canada

Caitlin Press Inc. acknowledges financial support from the Government of Canada
and the Canada Council for the Arts, and the Province of British Columbia through
the British Columbia Arts Council and the Book Publisher's Tax Credit.

LIBRARY AND ARCHIVES CANADA CATALOGUING IN PUBLICATION
Big : stories about life in plus-sized bodies / edited by Christina Myers.
Other titles: Stories about life in plus-sized bodies
Myers, Christina, editor.
Canadiana 20190192445 | ISBN 9781773860213 (softcover)
LCSH: Body image. | LCSH: Discrimination against overweight persons. | LCSH:
    Discrimination against overweight women. | LCSH: Overweight persons. |
    LCSH: Overweight women. | LCGFT: Essays.
LCC BF697.5.B63 B54 2019 | DDC 306.4/613—dc23

BIG

Stories about Life in
Plus-Sized Bodies

Edited by Christina Myers

CAITLIN PRESS

To the writers in this book, who are brave
and bold and full of magic

CONTENTS

INTRODUCTION

SOLID.

It was, so far as I can recall, the first word attributed to my body. It felt neutral and benign—a biological fact, not an emotional observation. In truth, I *was* solid. Strong and tall and built in a way that made me feel capable of anything I wanted or needed to do. I was the girl who could reach the top shelf and open jars and help teachers carry heavy boxes and outpace boys on the track and the tennis court.

On a bell curve of bodies, mine always fell somewhere outside the average—a little bit taller, a little bit broader, earlier to develop, faster to mature. But it worked for me. Solid wasn't an insult; it was an ideal, like the house built not of straw or twigs, but of bricks that could withstand a dangerous wolf outside its front door.

I didn't have the vocabulary or insight to say it as a child, but I felt at home in my body.

This was—as it is for many women—short-lived.

The safety I felt inside my body, the notion that my body and I coexisted in harmony, could not survive. In a world in which controlling and perfecting our bodies is the most important job, project, obsession and goal that a woman can have, it would have been impossible to reach the end of childhood feeling as benign and neutral about a word like *solid* as I did in the beginning.

Over time and for a million different reasons, *solid* became something to wish away—and eventually *solid* would be replaced by countless other words, attached to me by the culture I grew up in, by other people (both those I loved and strangers) and most of all by myself.

No one knows the power of words, of the words we use to describe bodies, more acutely than a woman who lives in a body that has been deemed imperfect and wrong because it is too big to fit into the very narrow definition of being the "right size."

What words do we use to define ourselves? What words do others use? Which of these are loving and which are hateful? Which words have stigma and which words can be reclaimed? Which words can be powerful and in what ways? Most of all, who decides?

I spent a lot of time thinking about these questions while working on this project, considering and reconsidering the implications of the words inside these pages and the words on the cover.

Why BIG, as a title? Why not large or fat, Rubenesque or zaftig? How about curvy, plus-sized, BBW? Maybe thick, or chubby, or chunky, or obese? Some speak to physical size, some to sexuality, some to medical textbook definitions, some to the ways we dress or live, some to how we view ourselves or are viewed by others, be they strangers or the most intimate of partners.

All of them fit, in one way or another, generally if not universally—but these words all mean different things to different people. And, maybe more importantly, the words we use often mean less to us in their actual definitions than in the way in which we *use* them.

As an adult, I had gotten in the habit of describing myself as *sturdy*. My body had changed over the years. The bookends of puberty and motherhood had altered it the most, along with genetics and a rotating carousel of diets and philosophies that vacillated between self-loathing and self-love. I have been a size 14 and a size 24, and everything in between—more than once. But I've always remained, physically and emotionally, solid: still the tall girl, the strong girl, the capable girl. I was and am proud of all the things I could do with my body because it was built this way. Calling myself *sturdy* felt safe, a variation on a theme; like its sister, *solid*, it was a word that was neutral compared with other possible words, most of which felt loud or controversial or, worst of all, shameful.

"I'm sturdy," I'd say, usually with a wink or chuckle. "I'd have made a great farm wife—big child-bearing hips, strong enough to pull a plow, I'd just work hard all day toting water and chopping wood."

It was a false front: a feigned implication that I embraced my body, under the guise of vague words and a dash of humour.

It wasn't until someone close to me called me out on it, several times, that I was forced to re-evaluate what I really meant—and, by extension, what I really thought.

"The way you say that is not kind to yourself," they said. "You don't mean it in a good way."

I hated to admit it, but they were right. And it wasn't the word itself—it was the way I used it, a masquerade of self-acceptance.

But I'm also keenly aware that someone else, using the same word in a different way, would have an entirely different intent, an entirely different tone, an entirely different meaning.

So what words, then, should I use? What words should any of us use? It is not an uncommon question these days, but the decision is ultimately so personal that I'm not convinced there is a right or best answer. What honours one person does not honour another, and removing a word from the cultural context in which it exists is more or less possible from one person to another, largely in relation to our own privileges or lack of them. We are too great a mix of our own intersections—the ways our personal histories, our families, our memories, our race, our genders, our sexual identities, our relationships and our communities have shaped us are so distinct and unique—to ever be on the same page, at the same time, about what words are the best.

Big is a simple word, with complicated implications. It is always a relative term, dependent on the unspoken comparison of something that is *not as big*. It is, in some ways, the most encompassing word, the most inclusive of experiences—because we can be (and are) big, in countless different ways. In choosing it as the title for this book, it is also intended as an invitation—an open-ended word that will resonate with readers in diverse definitions.

In the following pages are more than two dozen stories about being big—or fat, curvy, plus-sized, chubby and, yes, sturdy. Stories that each use the same words in very different ways. Stories that share small windows into what it means to live in a certain kind of body. Stories about childhood, bullying, sex, fashion, motherhood, health care, relationships, bodies, self-image. Stories that are funny or full of grief, or both. Stories that needed to be told and now need to be heard.

In creating this book, I was interested in curating a diversity of opinions and ideas and memories and views. It is not my job, or anyone's, to tell a person how they must feel about their own body. The writers in this collection are not a homogeneous group who all feel the same way about themselves, or about the culture and world that their bodies live in. While there are overlapping threads and common themes, these stories are a reflection of unique lived experiences and differing perspectives.

All of these writers, however, have this in common: in sharing these stories, they are vulnerable and honest and bold and brave. I am grateful for their passion and enthusiasm for this project.

To the reader holding this book in your hand right now: I hope these stories resonate with you in ways that are both familiar and brand new. I hope you learn something about other people and about yourself. Most of all, I hope this book makes you ask questions: about the way you think and talk about your own body and other people's bodies, about the world we live in and its lessons and obsessions, and about the words we use and how they shape us.

— Christina Myers

EUGENICS

Layla Cameron

"My sense of humour, compassionate nature, radical politics and values would all be different ... if I hadn't moved through the world as a fat person."

I COME FROM A FAMILY COMPOSED LARGELY OF MEDICAL PROFES-sionals. This is fantastic when you're a hypochondriac like I am, because there is always someone a phone call away to reassure you that you are, in fact, not dying of a heart attack, and that it is probably just acid reflux.

My family is also not the type of group to shy away from con-troversial subjects. I once had a friend tell me that my family's conversations over Christmas dinner were unlike any she had heard before. We don't particularly care about the weather or other mun-dane topics that tend to come up in casual conversation. We like to get into the nitty-gritty of hot-button social issues, such as the trash fire that is the current American political climate, recreational drug use as treatment for various mental health conditions, and even eugenics.

Almost ten years ago, I engaged in a conversation with some family members about whether or not it was morally acceptable—even desirable—to detect so-called "deficiencies" during pregnancy. We debated for a while about the moral and ethical implications of genetically modifying one's child, and about the rapid move-ment toward creating designer babies in which you could not only supposedly select the sex but also perhaps one day decide whether or not this person would be good at piano or long-distance running.

As the conversation escalated, I asked them a difficult question. If they had known how being fat would affect my life, would they have taken the opportunity to deselect "fat" from the panel of characteristics possessed by the little embryo that was to be me?

The answer was "Yes. Absolutely."

I was shocked, but I understood what they were saying: being fat had been the source of a lot of pain growing up, and they would have done what they could to protect me from that.

However, being fat had also shaped almost everything about me. My sense of humour, compassionate nature, radical politics and values would all be different, I was sure, if I hadn't moved through the world as a fat person. I was hurt that attempting to avoid the sometimes harsh reality of being fat was apparently worth the risk of gambling my entire existence.

THIS RESPONSE IS CERTAINLY NOT UNIQUE: 11 PERCENT OF MARried couples say they would abort a child if it were predisposed to "obesity."[1] That's just over one in ten.

And of course, fatness has not been the only target of eugenics movements. Eugenics efforts as we understand them now have been promoted for over a century, while elements of selective mating behaviours designed to breed out certain traits can be traced back to ancient Greece.

The consequences of these efforts are felt predominantly by those who occupy non-normative bodies. Medical science has sought to provide evidence of the natural inferiority of these bodies,

---

1. Kathleen LeBesco, *Revolting Bodies? The Struggle to Redefine Fat Identity* (Amherst, MA: University of Massachusetts Press, 2004), 59.

particularly for women and people of colour.[2] Forced sterilization has been imposed on people with disabilities, people of colour and poor people. Today, still, there are efforts to identify the "gay gene"; while this may be to solidify the argument that gay people are "born this way," the potential consequences of this are troubling. What do we plan to do with that information once, or if, we have it?

The quest to discover the causes of fatness is certainly connected to the medical exploration of disability, race, sexuality and class; after all, fat stigma is deeply interwoven with racism, classism, sexism, homophobia and (dis)ableism. All eugenics movements seek to achieve the same results: to eradicate "undesirable" states of being (largely those that threaten capitalism) and, ultimately, to rid the world of difference. Kathleen LeBesco acknowledges this desire for conformity by referring to these efforts as a "new consumer eugenics movement aimed at abolishing aberrations [deemed] socially or aesthetically undesirable (but far from life threatening)."[3]

Eradicating fatness in the name of health reigns strong in popular opinion despite growing evidence that suggests being fat is not life threatening. We are all encouraged to perform "good" health behaviours, and collectively we now have a moral and ethical responsibility to uphold normative health standards not only for our own well-being but also seemingly for that of the entire population. Claims that "obesity" is on par with terrorism as a threat to national security,[4] or that fat people have a significantly larger impact on the

2. Amy Erdman Farrell, *Fat Shame: Stigma and the Fat Body in American Culture* (New York: NYU Press, 2011), 65–66.

3. Kathleen LeBesco, "Quest for a Cause: The Fat Gene, the Gay Gene, and the New Eugenics," in *The Fat Studies Reader*, eds. Esther Rothblum and Sondra Solovay (New York: NYU Press, 2009), 65.

4. Natalie Boero, *Killer Fat: Media, Medicine, and Morals in the American "Obesity Epidemic"* (New Brunswick, NJ: Rutgers University Press, 2012).

environment or use more than their fair share of resources, support the moral panic that drives anti-fat sentiments in the name of collective action and patriotism. Would an obedient bio-citizen therefore participate in these eugenics efforts? Is being fat unethical?[5]

As people begin living longer than ever before in human history, public health priorities are shifting from curing disease to preventing disease, constructing the body as a project even before we enter the world and maintaining our anxieties about our bodies once we are here. We are a constant work in progress throughout our entire lives.

The mainstream "anti-obesity" movement, beginning in the 1990s—the same time I was born—labelled fatness as a disease to justify the amount of money spent on research and treatment, making it easier to access weight-loss resources and interventions as they were developed.[6] One such example is the effort to develop an inoculation against fatness, lovingly referred to as the "flab jab," that aims to make people immune to gaining weight, much as we are able to make people immune to infectious diseases such as measles.

I find it interesting that this medical response to fatness is contradictory to much of the medical research on the "obesity epidemic." If the spread of "obesity" is the result of poor lifestyle choices, laziness or the destruction of healthy food systems, then regardless of one's biological makeup, we are all at risk of becoming "obese."

---

5. No, it is not. As Christopher Mayes argues in *The Biopolitics of Lifestyle: Foucault, Ethics and Healthy Choices* (New York: Routledge, 2016), there is no empirical evidence to suggest that being fat is the result of individual choices. Further reading on the social determinants of health, or the numerous resources fat people do not have access to, negates these arguments. There is, however, plenty of evidence to show that fat stigma negatively impacts health and that fat people are subject to unethical and degrading treatment in a variety of areas.

6. Farrell, *Fat Shame*.

And, hypocritically, wouldn't the flab jab or other medical weight-loss interventions be not only an ineffective solution (given our "obesogenic" environment) but also a lazy one at that?

Fatness seems to resist all attempts to obliterate it. If diets worked, we would see success rates over 5 percent.[7] If weight-loss surgeries did not have serious complications (including fatal malnutrition),[8] more people would go under the knife. It makes sense, then, that those who see being fat as a problem, as a threat, as an economic drain, would want to get rid of the problem in utero, before it has a chance to infiltrate the world.

Once we're here, we don't seem to go away.

MY DISCOMFORT AROUND THE MEDICAL AND SCIENTIFIC approaches to fatness intensified as I began to navigate the medical system for a series of worrisome symptoms. It started in January 2017, when I first noticed that I could hear the pulsing of my heartbeat in my right ear. I had just returned from a trip for which I flew to my destination and had also recently had a sinus infection, so my doctor and I initially thought that my ear might simply be plugged. For the next two weeks, I pinched my nostrils shut and tried to blow air out of my nose in an attempt to pop my ear open. No luck.

It was determined that I had developed pulsatile tinnitus, a condition in which the heartbeat is heard as a whooshing sound. I describe it as listening to the heartbeat of a fetus during an ultrasound, but constantly, with no relief. When I push on the vein on the right side of my neck, the sound stops. There is no cure for pulsatile

7. Pat Lyons, "Prescription for Harm: Diet Industry Influence, Public Health Policy, and the 'Obesity Epidemic,'" in *The Fat Studies Reader*, eds. Esther Rothblum and Sondra Solovay (New York: NYU Press, 2009), 75.

8. Zimdars, *Watching Our Weights*, 27.

tinnitus; rather, it is a symptom of a condition that must be identified and treated. Common causes include a tumour, aneurysm or narrowing of the veins in the neck and head.

Over the next two years, I underwent numerous blood tests, MRI scans, a CT scan and a fantastic fluorescein angiogram that made me vomit immediately and violently into the cardboard tray kindly held out by the attending nurse. I was told I might have multiple sclerosis or a brain tumour. All of these tests came back negative; all indicated that I was in optimal health.

A lumbar puncture determined that, while my spinal fluid was clear, the opening pressure was high. This indicated that the pulsatile tinnitus was likely a symptom of a condition called idiopathic intracranial hypertension (IIH). IIH mimics the symptoms of a brain tumour due to the overproduction of spinal fluid. The "idiopathic" part of the name infers that the causes are unknown; however, as it is more common in "overweight" women, weight is assumed to be a contributing factor. Alas, because it tends to occur more often in women and in those who are "overweight," there is little research on this condition.

The neuro-ophthalmologist who requested the lumbar puncture, who to this day has never asked me what my weight is or what my lifestyle is like, continued at every appointment to encourage me to lose 10 percent of my body weight and become more active.[9] She made assumptions about my diet and level of activity by looking at the size of my body. I feel confident that this would not have happened if I had been thin.

I was prescribed a drug that the doctor commented was "luckily also an appetite suppressant" and is a diuretic, and whose side effects include vomiting. It continues to amaze me that we encourage the

9. I laugh and laugh (and cry) when medical professionals suggest weight loss as if this were something a fat person had never considered before.

embodiment of disordered eating habits—medical conditions that we recognize as being extremely harmful to the body—to fat people, as if one's fatness were more dire than the physical and psychological consequences of anorexia or bulimia.

I took the medication and smiled and nodded at the neuro-ophthalmologist while she told me to be more active, mentally trying to figure out where to fit more exercise in my schedule between playing softball four times a week, swimming, yoga classes, hiking and walking my dog numerous times a day.

The psychological consequences of these medical experiences are not unlike those of living in the world as a fat person: we begin to hate ourselves, disassociate from our bodies and neglect to treat ourselves with love, kindness and compassion. I have read that a consequence of fat stigma is that "the fat body is effectively rendered uninhabitable."[10] I will not deny that the additional mental, emotional and physical labour it requires to survive in this world while fat is exhausting.

THE EFFECTS OF LIVING IN A WORLD THAT IS TRYING TO MOVE your community toward extinction are severe. Fat people experience discrimination in the workplace, when attempting to build a family and through social isolation. Fat people are more likely to experience medical negligence, are less likely to be married and receive less encouragement to apply to college.

I sound defensive, and that's because I am.

I am not here to argue about the benefits of physical activity or nutrition. I will, however, defend my position that the medical care fat people receive is of significantly lesser quality than what non-fat people receive, that weight stigma and fat bias permeate every

10. LeBesco, *Revolting Bodies?*, 3.

institution and facet of our daily lives, and that the medical industry is perhaps the one area that causes the most irreversible harm. It is medical and scientific research that is working to wipe us from this earth, and yet we hang on, resilient as ever and apparently growing in numbers of epidemic proportions. We are a moral panic masked as a public health crisis; the world is getting fatter, and we are scared.

Regardless of this cultural fear, I cannot ever imagine looking at my child and telling them that I would have changed them if I could, that perhaps everything would be easier if I had changed something about them that realistically (and statistically) will never change.

I don't think that was the intention of the conversation I had with my family, either. What I think this conversation revealed is the unfortunate reality of growing up fat in North America, and the difficult decisions parents have to make to protect their children from serious harm. This is what happens when a society refuses to fit its people and instead insists that its people fit into its suffocating and falsely rigid boundaries of what is normal and what is not.

Would I choose to change my child if it turned out that they, too, were going to be fat? I would not be able to guarantee that I could protect them from a world that hates their body. I would not be able to ensure that their inevitable restrictive eating habits in adolescence would not turn into a full-blown disorder in adulthood, or that they would be able to brush off daydreams of self-harm, or that they would be able to rise above their bullies instead of turning into one themselves.

What I do know is this: I wouldn't change myself or my fatness, and, for now, that is enough of an answer for me.

PRECIPITATION

Rabbit Richards

"I never actually touch anyone else, but people react to my passing as if they need to check themselves for damage."

I'M WALKING UP MAIN FROM ALEXANDER TO THE SKYTRAIN STA-tion to go stare at the water behind Science World. The tops of the mountains are cloaked in fog. The seagulls are bleating like goats, fighting over bits of bread cast from upper-storey windows. The air is warm but the rain is cold and the dissonance makes me want blankets and tea, but at least when it rains you don't smell as much of what's being washed away.

I don't romanticize petrichor the way I see other poets do, although it is a good smell. It's just that in the Downtown Eastside rain is more cover noise and garden hose, less idyllic concept. I'm new to Skwxwú7mesh and still haven't figured out appropriate rain gear. Mostly I wear soft hoodies, let them get soaked through and have several stages of drying clothes hanging on a line in my apartment.

I've had one raincoat in my life that I loved, and it was when I was about six years old. It was reversible: a lavender slicker on one side and the textured side featuring the signature floral print from Bonwit Teller. I wore it until it was so small on me that it pinched the flesh on the insides of my armpits, even in the summer with just a thin cotton shirt underneath. The hood was big enough for my fluffy hair, and I felt like Fashion in it because it came from the same store Katharine Hepburn shopped at in *Desk Set*.

Never mind that the store had lost a lot of its glamour between *Breakfast at Tiffany's* and the 1980s. Donald Trump had that effect on many things in my city, and Fifth Avenue and Fifty-Sixth Street was a place my mother took me, to get coffee (for her) and to disappear in racks of luxurious leather goods and diaphanous scarves that cost the same as our car (for me). She was always careful to tell me to use the good bathrooms but make eye contact with no one unless it was direct. If I ever saw "the Donald" in the hallways I was to make myself invisible and come straight back to her.

Thinking about that raincoat always makes me feel like I've grown too big for my bones. Last year I bought a winter coat from Torrid, mail order from the States. I was shocked at its quality, because clothes my size are almost always flimsy and poorly constructed. (The buttons keep falling off, but in this economy, who expected otherwise?) I did have one good coat when I was living in Kelowna a decade ago, but at the time I had much different supports, and my body, while still considered "plus-sized," fit in the largest size they made at Cleo.

I told everyone that was the first coat I ever had that made me feel feminine, but it was also the first coat I ever had that fit, at least since that little lavender raincoat. And it made me feel invisible in good ways. Like I could blend in. I didn't cut the size tag off, as I often do so that when the coat is hanging on a hook anonymously I don't have to hear skinny people tittering about how stressful it would be if they ever owned anything with that many Xs on it.

PEOPLE JOSTLE FOR PLACE AT MAIN AND HASTINGS, AND I AM keenly aware of how much space I need to slip between people who are standing mostly still but who also weave unexpectedly through the streets. I get stopped a lot because I wear my hair in brightly coloured box braids. I don't always love the attention, but it does mitigate some of the ways people look at me. I can see the irritation on their faces before they switch to some variation of OMG YOUR HAIR IS AMAAAAAAZING, and to be honest it's not the worst way I've distracted people from being annoyed at my physical presence.

When I grew from a sickly child to an unhealthy teen, my body changed from boyish to mannish, with the sole exception of enormous breasts. (I was using she/her pronouns then, and no one in my life had been made to question this.) Being seen as an object of desire in a game that wasn't just about power was very disconcerting to me, but I also really liked being seen as feminine. It's a tricky line, being the biggest girl on the gymnastics team. Being "big and strong" was like stealing attributes from someone else's character sheet. Being stared at for my chest seemed like a dangerous way to finally be seen as something other than the sick weird kid in the corner. Being became difficult in a new way.

I've seen a photo of myself at age fourteen, all elbows and knees and a plastified smile. I remember feeling fat the day the picture was taken. I remember feeling fat always. I don't know where the photo had been buried, but when I pulled it out of my mother's bureau drawer, tears came immediately. I was so thin you could see the shapes of my long bones. I had a swollen belly because my digestion was so messed up. I could look at the face of that child and know it was me, even as I remembered that the morning of that day I had wanted to choose different clothes and my mother had overruled me. Remembered wanting simultaneously to disappear and to be a star. To be seen and to be left alone. It rained that day, too. I think I wore a T-shirt and pretended I didn't care.

There was a long succession of hand-me-down jackets and outerwear, most of which came from the men in my family. I have broad shoulders, which I am told helps me look more "balanced," but that means none of the women in my family have clothes I can borrow. (I know there is no way I am the only non-binary person in my family, but I'm the only one I know of. Not so much invisible as hypervisible, like everywhere else.)

In college I wore anything I could afford from the men's section of Old Navy or H&M. I was lucky enough to live in Brooklyn near Kings Plaza mall, one of the few that housed plus-size sections in the department stores and where I could actually try clothes on instead of waiting for them to arrive in the mail. People complimented my style, but what they mostly meant was that I was doing a good job of fitting sideways into compartments not created for me.

THEY PUT A COMMUNITY GARDEN UNDER THE GEORGIA VIADUCT. On wet days it smells of mulch and weeds. I've seen the occasional squash leaf in there, but usually the boxes of earth look empty and sad. I think a lot about planting there, but would I trust to eat the food that came from it? And isn't the lack of green—both vegetables and spaces—carefully planned out? The cars speed through that section of Main Street and it's a dangerous intersection for pedestrians. My understanding is that the only reason the viaduct isn't farther north is down to community organizing in Chinatown. Vancouver decided to erase the black neighbourhood instead. If you know who to ask or how to see it, there are bits and pieces of history everywhere. There's someone in the garden today, but it's hard to tell if it's someone who's there to garden or someone who's there to touch soil for a moment or someone who's there because there aren't a lot of places to be that don't feel like you shouldn't be there at all.

I DON'T BOTHER TAKING A BUS UP TO MAIN STREET–SCIENCE World. It's always crowded in the stretch up to the station, and I need to sit down but don't "look" disabled. I'd rather walk and be wet and tired than explain that, while I don't seem frail or like I might waste away, I am fragile and need care. Fat people aren't afforded care. Fat people are judged morally for existing in our bodies, and then snubbed because our relative health is our own responsibility and has nothing to do with consumer capitalism or a childhood soaked in stress hormones.

Fat black people are supposed to know their place and disappear. Fat neurodivergent people are in the way. Fat Jewish people don't exist. I'm aware of the ways oppression intersects over my head and creates a grid of lasers I don't fit in. I can walk instead. Lucky me. Today. On days when I'm not able to walk, I get to face drivers who look at me disappointedly or refuse outright when I ask for the bus to kneel.

Under the station, I dip round the corner to the Tim's. Like my mom, I prefer my coffee piping hot, preferably black. She taught me to order a larger-sized coffee than I actually want to drink, so it stays hot in the cup longer. This was especially useful when we were getting the coffee on the way home from the city, to take the long express bus ride back home to Canarsie. Cold coffee comforts no one and doesn't really accompany stashed salami sandwiches very well.

But now I order coffee in front of thin white hipster women, and I wonder if my mother was aware of the size of her hips when she ordered hers. I wonder if saying *extra large* will ever feel less like pulling a spotlight directly over my own head. I wait in front of the Pick Up Here sign and try to shake some of the water from my hood without making too much of a mess.

Dipping out from under the station, I make my way through holes in the commuter crowd. I never actually touch anyone else, but people react to my passing as if they need to check themselves for damage. I don't look back, but I hear people make comments behind my back. A lot of assumptions get made about where fat comes from.

About how a fat person "got that way" or why they're out in public where the thin can see them or are in some way forced to interact. I prefer the way the rain invades my personal space. It's not consensual either, but it isn't singling me out for special notice.

I dodge the weird statues of people at café tables in front of the Science World plaza. Sit on a bench and stare out at the water, and across it to the homes of people who can afford a waterfront view in the middle of a housing crisis. Sip my coffee and let the rainwater from the lid dilute it in my mouth. The sun has glared between cracks in the clouds until the fog has burned off, and the rain makes a steady sort of soft curtain. By the time I get home, my hoodie will be twice its own weight. I'll hang it on the line in the living room and switch to the next one, and try not to see this process as metaphorical.

EASY OUT

Simone Blais

"That's when I spotted him: the right fielder playing close to the infield, betting the fat girl at the plate would lightly tap a high fly ball."

I WAS FOOLED INTO THINKING IT WAS A CONVENTIONAL CLINIC. Beige walls, brittle vinyl blinds, speckled ceiling tiles like dusty feta cheese. As I stared up at the fluorescent lights, the banality of this room provided comfort, assured me that acupuncture would be like any other medical treatment.

The doctor placed three fingers on the inside of my upper thigh, rotating this triangle of assessment clockwise, counter-clockwise, seemingly measuring the height and width of an imaginary organ hanging from my joint. I was about to tell him that it was my ankle that hurt when, without warning, he jabbed his thumb down into the fleshy part of my knee. Blinded by pain, I cried out in between gasps for breath.

"It hurts because you're fat," he announced with a perfunctory air. Salt water brimmed my eyes as he lifted my leg into his armpit and dug deeper still.

GROWING UP, MY IDENTITY HAD ALWAYS BEEN TIGHTLY WOVEN into the uniforms I wore—basketball singlets, track shorts, baseball jerseys. Performing at competitive levels meant perpetual practices, early morning training or three-day tournaments. Family get-togethers rarely involved questions about boys in my life; queries revolved around the past sports season, what I was currently playing, and training for the season to come.

My true love turned out to be softball. I was called up for my first provincial championship at eight years old. As a scrawny late-season pickup, I sat most of the games but managed to hit the game-winning run in the final. I beamed, and friends still tell the story of how my dad bounded along the foul line cheering. We were both hooked.

I played through high school and college and into adulthood, transitioning to slo-pitch leagues in my twenties. I had good intentions of dialing it down a notch to focus on a career. Hitting long fly balls, though, quickly caught the eye of team managers—and I was recruited to competitive squads with aspirations of national titles.

I balanced the training and competition with a sedentary day job, which allowed space to play one or two games a night. No longer the scrappy youngster, I shopped for XL tops and plus-sized bottoms that could accommodate my thick quads and glutes. I noticed that as I gained, I grew stronger: throwing my weight behind an inside pitch lifted the ball higher and longer than before, propelled throws to first at increasing speeds, froze runners in their tracks in a never-say-die stance over the base.

My male teammates described my strength and tenacity to others with pride. "She's like a dude," they'd say on the sidelines.

That description always made me smile.

IN THE SEASON LEADING UP TO THE NATIONAL CHAMPIONSHIPS, more tournaments were added to the team's packed schedule. The strategy was to elevate the level of play incrementally, testing endurance, stamina and strength. It also tested my left Achilles heel, which became a nagging pain packed with my gear no matter what field we played on.

Opposing teams would laugh at our lineup: male batters saw two ladies on the same side of the infield as an invitation. Our coach devised it as a trap. At first glance, Kate and I should have been switched around on the field. She was the lithe and graceful second baseman who made any play look seamless with her bounding strides. Height is usually reserved for first base, but I had an uncanny ability to stretch out into the splits, which served the shortstop well when he blew the throw to one. Kate and I were a deceptive and lethal combination.

After one Saturday morning game, I limped off the field as Kate watched, frowning. Athletes play through the pain; there's no phoning in sick to slo-pitch. The only thing that will get you out of games is a cast—and even then, you better need crutches to get around. Ball bags carried a range of ointments, bandages, braces and medications on any given weekend. But she could tell my ankle was heading to crutches and quick. She recommended I try acupuncture; she went to someone in Vancouver who blends sports medicine with acupuncture, using the needle to tease the muscle out of tightness. The next day you feel like you've been hit by a Mack truck, she explained, but it would loosen up and running would be a breeze.

No more pain. Freedom to play. It was an offer I couldn't turn down.

I WAS TORN BETWEEN GOING TO KATE'S SPECIALIST AND HAVING the visit covered under benefits. The pocketbook won out, so I had to go to someone registered with the College of Traditional Chinese Medicine Practitioners and Acupuncturists. It wasn't sports medicine, but I crossed my fingers, trusting relief would be only a few pinpricks away.

The clinic was set up in a converted heritage house, and I met the doctor in his office. He was behind his desk, a giant slab of oak surrounded by wood panelling. He seemed friendly enough, in a reserved kind of way. Sitting opposite me, he asked why I booked the appointment. I described the pain in my heel and ankle, and the shooting pains that throbbed even while I slept.

He didn't ask how it happened. Nor did he ask me to describe the pain, where it was located or what movement caused aggravation. He sat quietly, hands folded in his lap. I filled the void by explaining that it was a softball injury that reappeared consistently when I tried to run the bases.

He cut me off abruptly. "How much do you weigh?"

I paused a second, wondering if I had said something to trigger the question. I told him a number.

"How long have you been carrying this weight around?" As though it were luggage I should have checked with the valet. Doubts began to seep into my mind.

He told me that pain of all sorts would torment me as long as I was overweight, but that I was fortunate in that he had methods that would be able to treat me. Looking back, it was unclear whether he meant my ankle or my waistline.

I was brought to a clinical-looking room and told to lie down on the paper-wrapped table. After grabbing my knee, he started the treatment not in my ankle but in my hand—spreading my fingers open to slide needles deeply into my palm. He drained a bruise on my leg by puncturing the skin with a stapler-type device, creating small holes from multiple needles. Then he placed a cup and vacuumed the skin, leaving the blood to leak out. I sat with both ankles in this suctioned state, unable to move my lower or upper body for fear of dislodging the apparatuses affixed to my extremities. I tried to ask what he was doing and received only muttered replies. Without much explanation of what was happening or how these methods would work, I was left to imagine. *Stay positive*, I told myself. *This worked for Kate, so it's got to work for you, too.*

After a spell, he returned to the room and disassembled the various appliances and pulled the needles from my body. He motioned for me to follow him to a spacious room down the hall, filled with white pod-style beds that looked like they belonged in a space station. "Drink this, and then you lie back here." I was handed a cup of tea and instructed to gulp it down. Then I was wrapped in a silvery foil and locked into the capsule, where the heat cooked me like a cased sausage. I wondered if there was a drain tray where the fat would go.

Left to my own devices for what felt like an eternity, I finally flagged down a medical tech who came in the room and asked her to pop open the capsule. I put my clothes back on and hustled out—sweaty, confused and still in pain.

SHOULD HAVE KNOWN BETTER. THE THOUGHT STUCK IN MY HEAD like a shard of glass as I drove back to work. I had no business blaming myself, and yet that thought fragment nicked me, digging into my mind.

I vacillated between anger and confusion, torn between white-hot rage (*did I just pay to be a pincushion?*) and the quicksand of shame and embarrassment. Back in the office, I avoided making eye contact so people wouldn't see my flushed cheeks. Humiliation wasn't exactly a foreign feeling; I grew up with a Catholic mother who weaponized guilt with exacting precision. But this felt different, like I had been caught committing a crime.

Settling in my cubicle, I noted for the first time how the arms of the chair dug into my hips. Everything around me felt heavy and swollen, as though my chair and desk would collapse under the weight of my thudding heart. I was lost in swirling thoughts. Should I have stopped him, left the clinic? I should have walked out of the room. Did staying in place mean I consented to being treated that way? Did I deserve that treatment?

My voice ran from the cage of my large frame, and I could only mumble my way through the rest of the day, in a fog—a dense, degrading fog that lingered.

I WOKE THE NEXT DAY WITH HEAT RADIATING FROM MY ANKLE. Kate's promise came true; I did feel like I had been run over by a Mack truck. That pain didn't emanate from muscles but from the realization that my slender teammate would have had a different health-care experience from my own. This reality burned more than the grated skin on the back of my leg.

She asked what I thought about acupuncture, and all I could bring myself to say was how he jammed needles in my hand, not my ankles. I made light of it, joked about surviving a torturous experience and how the cure was worse than the disease.

My halting gait continued unabated. It took a few months before I could open up to anyone about what happened, and it was to the person least likely to understand weight stigma. My sister had always been smaller than the kids her age. Her tiny physique rounded slightly in puberty and remained acceptably curvy throughout adulthood. I recounted the experience, bracing for what she would say. Her reaction was visceral.

"That's bullshit," she pronounced. "What a dick. Don't listen to him."

I breathed easier on her definitive assessment, but something was still nagging me—the searing pain in my ankle, or the sliver in my mind.

I LACED UP MY CLEATS FOR AN EVENING MATCHUP AGAINST THE
Jays. Far from the Toronto MLB franchise, they were friendly adver-
saries in league play, always good for lively banter. We were scoreless
heading into the third inning when I had my first at-bat. I eyed up the
field for options to move the runners around. Bases were loaded, so
the infield had moved in to try to make a play at home plate. There
wasn't a lot of room in the infield to manoeuvre, adding to my nerves.

From the sideline, my coach gave me a knowing look. That's
when I spotted him: the right fielder playing close to the infield, betting the fat girl at the plate would lightly tap a high fly ball. Given
how often we played this team, they should know me by now, respect
my skills—not treat me as an easy out.

"You got this," my coach said with a nod.

I grinned, digging into the batter's box as doubt slipped away.
That's right, I thought, as I swooped the bat around with two slow
practice swings. *It'll go far because I'm fat.*

THE SWIMSUIT

Jo Jefferson

---

*"Now, instead of feeling ashamed of my body, I feel
disappointed in myself for having ignored it for so long."*

TEN YEARS AFTER HER DEATH, MY MOTHER'S OLD SPEEDO IS STILL
my only swimsuit. Modest navy blue, wide in the thighs and butt,
sturdy and practical. It reminds me of her. I've been hanging on to
it for far too long—because I dread clothes shopping of any kind,
because I don't know how to find the kind of swimsuit that will
actually feel right for my body and my gender, because deep down I
don't believe that I deserve to have anything better. But this year, I've
decided it's time to stop wearing my mother's hand-me-down. This
year, before outdoor swimming season starts, I'm finally going to get
myself a new swimsuit.

I've always been a swimmer. My parents used to joke-brag about
needing to stop at every swimming hole on every family trip. During
our summer cross-country road trip in 1973, the year I turned ten, I
kept a journal in which I recorded every swimming pool and beach I
swam at with my sister.

I don't know what my bathing suit looked like that year, but it
was probably a Speedo or a cheaper copy (my mother was frugal and
objected to paying extra for a brand name). Definitely not a two-piece.
Those were for girls. I couldn't have said that out loud, even to myself,
at the time, but I think that's how I felt, with or without the words for

it. Also, I have a feeling my mother thought bikinis were impractical and inappropriate.

The next summer, I went to Big Cove YMCA Camp for the first time. We swam off a dock in Merigomish Harbour—deep, cold, salty water full of jellyfish. One trip around the harbour was a 1.6-kilometre swim. I have a clear memory of eleven-year-old me walking into the camp dining hall, late for supper, the day I swam five times around the harbour. Eight kilometres. Only one other kid, a bigger boy, did it that day. I don't remember any kind of medal or certificate I might have been awarded, but I do remember thinking that the whole camp was watching me, impressed. It didn't matter that I wasn't a fast swimmer. I had endurance. I was tough.

Swimming was something I took pretty seriously. Lessons every year. Lifeguard qualifications. Summer camp waterfront jobs. My seasons revolved around indoor and outdoor swimming spaces: Green Bay, Rissers Beach, Cavendish Beach, Susies Lake, Merigomish Harbour, The Dingle, North River, Shortts Lake, Lake Banook, Chocolate Lake, Williams Lake, Long Lake, Centennial Pool, Waegwoltic Club, YMCA, YWCA.

Why was swimming such a big deal for me? Maybe for the same reason writing was. I got praised for it, I felt confident doing it, I felt strong. I could do it by myself and didn't have to rely on or communicate with anyone else. Just put my head down, swim away and then look around and see people smiling and impressed when I dried off. And it wasn't something that depended on any specific gender. I had swimming heroes who were women: Nancy Garapick won two bronze medals at the 1976 Olympics in Montreal, swam at the same pool I did and was only two years older than me. And some who were men: Graham Smith won six gold medals at the 1978 Commonwealth Games in Edmonton. I cut both their pictures out of the newspaper and taped them on my bedroom wall next to my pictures of Secretariat and Luke Skywalker.

My mother wasn't a serious swimmer until late in her life. When I was a kid she would go in for a short dip at the oceanside cottage we rented every summer. She always swam parallel to the surf in a slow, dignified breaststroke with her face above the surface, sometimes with a flowery bathing cap on her head. Mostly, though, the cottage beach was a walking or sitting and reading place. I have a photo of the two of us sitting near each other on the sand, both immersed in books, both wearing long shorts, wide-brimmed hats and extra-large sweatshirts.

Later, my mother became a disciplined long-distance pool swimmer, even getting serious enough to start putting her face in the water for a diligent and plodding front crawl. She wore goggles and a tight bathing cap over her hair. That's when she started wearing a Speedo, carefully rinsing the chlorine out of it after every swim so the suit wouldn't degrade too quickly. She wanted to get her money's worth.

I had always thought of her as a heavy woman. She fretted about her shape, I knew, and carefully chose styles of clothes to de-emphasize the aspects of her body that she wasn't comfortable with. I think I heard her complain more about her "mousy, flat hair" than about her size, but she watched her weight, ate a lot of cottage cheese and baked us all bran muffins. She warned me about eating too much ice cream and too many thick slices of her homemade bread, which I loved to slather with peanut butter and butter. Her own mother was thick of torso and always seemed somewhat shapeless to me, an affectionate, squishy, food-loving, solid-bodied grandmother.

I could have predicted my own future body shape by looking at the two of them. But as a kid, and later as an adolescent, I was known as the tall one, the skinny one, the one with the bottomless pit of an appetite.

My older brother's best friend was a lifeguard at Centennial Pool. His hair had that golden-green chlorine glow of people who spend most of their time in pools, and I thought he was the cutest guy. He was probably also my brother's first boyfriend, but I wasn't up to speed on that aspect of my family story—I was the baby and was never let in on any of the secrets. One day at the pool I swam up to the surface after a really solid dive off the high board, shook the drops of water off my head like a happy otter and glanced up to see him looking down at me, his flutter board tucked under one arm, eyebrows cocked in his teasing way. I grinned up at him, hoping my hair looked just like Nancy Garapick's did right after she finished setting a world record. He said, "Your brother was right. Your ears really do stick out."

I already knew I couldn't do anything about my stick-out ears, but I assumed I'd have a swimmer's body forever. Broad shoulders, narrow hips, smooth skin, short hair.

A few years later, at the same pool, I swam in a high school meet. I was lousy in my breaststroke heat, coming a slow last, embarrassed, breathless. My imposter status had been exposed—I wasn't actually a serious swimmer, not when it really counted. But a cute guy from my school flicked his towel at my legs and asked me out.

After high school I spent a summer as waterfront director for a church camp on Long Lake. I spent two months in the lake or on the dock, watching kids in the water, jumping out of canoes, practising rescues. I had to have two swimsuits so that there was always a dry one to put on for the next session at the waterfront, and I wore flip-flops all the time. I felt good, strong, tanned, fit and respected. Two of my best camp friends—guys I had gone to elementary school and Sunday school with—started calling me Iron Butt that summer. They said it with great affection, and I loved being given a hard-core nickname. I rationalized that it was about being badass, a take-no-shit leader. Everyone knew it was because I had a big butt. I scrutinized my full-body profile in the mirror, in store windows as I walked by, in pictures people took of me. I reminded myself constantly to stand with my butt tucked in, my tailbone curled in on itself trying to hide.

I thought about how big my butt was when I ate slabs of bread with peanut butter and bowl after bowl of ice cream.

Worrying about how my body looked in a swimsuit didn't become a real problem until after I had a baby. Maybe it was the overtly, inescapably female way my body felt and people saw me; maybe it was the extra fifty pounds I carried around by the end of my first pregnancy; maybe it was my purple stretch marks snaking down my thighs, which now suddenly seemed enormous, flapping and chafing whenever I was above the surface. Maybe it was because I could no longer just put my head down and swim until everyone else had left the changing room. Maybe it was the maternity swimsuit my mother had sewn for me. I kept on wearing it long after pregnancy was over, because it was still in my closet, it still fit, it was still holding together, and my mother made it for me.

Since the kids were too young to go in the water on their own, and swim time was a treat they shared only with me, and it was a way to get out of the house and get some exercise even in the middle of winter, I put my suit on to go in the water with them and covered myself with a towel whenever possible. Seeing all the other mothers at the pool, and all the lifeguards and team swimmers hanging around in swimsuits, reminded me of my own lost (imaginary) body. I was visible only as a mother. A mother in a swimsuit that exposed all the things I no longer liked about my former-swimmer's body.

We went to parent-and-tot swim programs and to my favourite childhood ocean swimming spots. I took them to the lake beaches around the city. We went to the Waegwoltic Club with my parents and watched Grandma do her daily kilometre-long swims in the saltwater pool. And eventually we moved to within a ten-minute drive of the best ocean beaches in the province—gorgeous soft sand and smooth curling surf. We spent hours in the waves from June to September. The kids were happy to be in the water or on the sand, and I was happy to be nearby, watching, away from the mothers who lay on the beach in their bikinis. I wore a T-shirt and shorts instead of a swimsuit. I stayed warmer that way, in the frigid, fog-chilled North Atlantic, and avoided too much sun exposure. Avoided too much exposure of the body that I now recognized was more obviously female than I felt on the inside.

Once I passed forty, it seemed like people stopped seeing me, so I stopped worrying about what I looked like. I reclaimed the pleasure of swimming for the sake of it. I pulled Mum's old swimsuit out of the closet and started wearing it again, even though it left my thighs bare and made my breasts seem more obvious and did nothing to hide my wide butt.

For a long time, that has been enough. I change into and out of it as quickly as possible, cover my thighs and belly with a towel as soon as I get out of the water and am careful to rinse out the salt or chlorine right away. I could keep swimming in this swimsuit until I die.

A lot has changed. I don't live near the ocean anymore. I'm co-parenting another kiddo. I'm out to lots of people as genderqueer. I have friends who celebrate their body size and shape—fat femmes who wear bikinis, trans folks with scars they're proud of—who flaunt their physical selves in front of other people. Now, instead of feeling ashamed of my body, I feel disappointed in myself for having ignored it for so long. I haven't done the work to really build a loving relationship with my physical self, to honour it in the way I've seen so many others do with their own bodies.

Now, heading for sixty and wanting to be a good role model of gender celebration and affirmation, I feel ready to do that work. Now, I want people to see me for who I am, in my body. Not a woman. Not a mother. Not a flabby introvert in an oversized T-shirt. When I'm at the city pool or at the lake, the cottage or the campground, or back in Nova Scotia in my beloved ocean waves, I want people to see a proud genderqueer human with a strong, sturdy swimmer's body.

So I think it's finally time to let Mum's swimsuit rest. But to do that, I have to get myself a new one, and if I'm going to finally do that for myself and spend that much money, I might as well get a swimsuit that I'm going to feel good about, right? One that feels great on my body and helps my body feel fabulous for me. My swimmer's body. Flappy thighs and triceps, saggy stretchy belly and flabby wide butt. Exactly as it needs to be, right now.

BARBRA STREISAND OR BUST!

Dr. Rohini Bannerjee

"There was an innocence in how my thick body looked and felt. ... I was the proof that they had succeeded as immigrant parents in Canada."

I AM NOT QUITE SURE EXACTLY HOW BIG I WAS AT BIRTH. MY mother will say I was nearly twelve pounds. She knew I would simply have to arrive on earth via Caesarean section.

"There was no way you were going to fit. I just knew it. All that strawberry shortcake I ate in my last trimester had caught up to me and, well, you."

Sure, I did look like a three-month-old infant at birth, lots of hair, almond-shaped eyes, full, round cheeks. But beyond the physical cuteness of being a chubby baby, I grew into my bubbly personality. As a toddler with my hairbrush in hand, circa 1977, I sang Barbra Streisand without any hesitation. My dad stood in for Neil Diamond, and our duet of "You Don't Bring Me Flowers" was always a show-stopper at dinner parties.

Look at those sweet cheeks!

Oh, she is a healthy, big girl. She fills out that frock so nicely.

She is growing up so quickly. Look how big she is getting.

Loving compliments, I assumed. I remember my parents admiring how "sturdy" I was, in sharp contrast to photos I saw of them from their childhood growing up in post-Partition India.

See how skinny we were? It was tough.

We were thin because there was not always enough dhal left in the pot, you know?

I was the youngest in my family, and a girl, so I got whatever was left.

Skinniness, for my South Asian parents, meant "not enough." And part of their mission to move to Canada in the late 1960s was to make sure their children never had to grow up like them. The plump, round, medium-skinned daughter was their ideal baby.

There was an innocence in how my thick body looked and felt when I ran to them for a hug. I was snuggly and warm, and to them, I was the proof that they had succeeded as immigrant parents in Canada.

As a five-year-old in school, my bubbly Streisand lip-synch moves evolved into chatterbox reading and socializing. I skipped kindergarten because of my ability to outdo my peers (and sometimes the teacher). My kind and empathetic principal wanted me in grade two, but my parents were hesitant and opted for grade one instead, concerned about the two-year age gap with my fellow students. I moved through my schoolwork quickly, and as a result, my penmanship might have suffered. I was bright and engaged, quick to learn, and I loved my teachers.

And then something happened. I noticed my uniform kilt was bigger than Anna's and Gina's. I noticed that my blouse buttons were close to popping, unlike Kirsten's and Jennifer's slimmer fits. I noticed Ameeta and Margie could do somersaults without hesitation, while my gym shorts didn't quite cover my thighs. I was nine years old and noticing my full, round body.

You have broad shoulders.

Look at that wide chest; hopefully you will be tall so it evens out.

If you had been a boy, you would have played football.

And then there was the layered haircut. I don't know what my mother was thinking, but I went to the local Head Shoppe hair salon chain and my hair was butchered. With only two boys in our class, one of whom, James, was of South Asian heritage like myself, I knew someone was going to think I was him now. *He eats with his mouth open and picks his nose and, well, is a boy!* I woke up the next morning, did nothing to my hair, felt a little weird about it not being in a ponytail or braid, scoffed down my usual sunny-side-up egg and brown wheat toast and made it to school.

You look like a boy.

Your face looks rounder.

I never noticed how round your nose is, kind of like a parrot beak.

I thought you were James.

And that was it. Not only were my full cheeks and thick nose feeling rounder than ever, my nightmare was now a reality: I looked like a boy; I looked like James. I managed to get through the day, quietly eating my Kraft Singles sandwich and Joe Louis cake at lunchtime, nibbling my Oreo cookie during after-school care, and got home.

THIS WAS A STANDARD WEEKNIGHT: DASHING ABOUT TO SET THE table, turning on *Three's Company* and eating together. Mum would be wearing her nursing uniform at dinner, and before we had a moment to digest, she would be out the door at 6:15 p.m. four nights a week to do her 7:00 p.m. to 7:00 a.m. nursing shift—a choice she had made upon the birth of her kids. Eating quickly but together was so that she could be with us for dinner, the only real time we were able to spend with her. Sometimes I ate so quickly my tongue would burn, but eating became a no-longer-pleasurable act; it was something I did to get *out* of social situations as my body became rounder and larger. Looking back, I did not sit and savour the flavour of the meals my mother so lovingly prepared for us. Surrounded by food, as quickly as I could, I plowed through my dinner plate, tandoori chicken, chapati, mint chutney and vegetable biryani, and said

I had tons of homework, once Mum had left and the kitchen was clean, closing my bedroom door, still a little nauseous from overeating without taking a breath, ready for a good cry.

That spunky, Barbra Streisand–singing, chatterbox kid grew silent. As my hair grew out, my cheeks, belly, arms and legs did too. I wanted to slip out of focus. I naturally, without much thought, muted my voice and did my best to disappear into the everyday routine of school.

MY MATERNAL UNCLE, A RETIRED MAJOR IN THE INDIAN ARMY, hosted family Sunday dinners nearly every weekend. I loved watching my older cousin Anjali put on her makeup, while my mum and aunt cooked dinner and my father and uncle watched the evening news. I watched her copy the Streisand cat eyeliner so precisely and outline her lips with a deep, crimson red, just like Tina Turner.

"You know ... you are a pretty girl. I am sure your baby fat will go away," she told me. My cousin was gorgeous, nine years my senior, with long, curly hair and a natural arch to her eyebrows Joan Jett could never quite get. If she said I was pretty, I must have been.

"Yeah, I don't know. I don't know if this is baby fat. I'm, like, twelve years old now."

Then my uncle finally said something.

"Beti, you are so quiet. Whenever you are here, you just disappear into Anjali's room and then come out, eat dinner and go back again. Are you some kind of monk or something?"

My cousins were shocked. My parents quickly intervened: "She's just shy. She's quite active in school; French is her best subject, and she recites poems daily to us. She's not active in sports, you know, just keeps to herself, reads books, does her homework, quiet."

I wanted to scream at the top of my lungs: I am not a monk. I am a girl with dreams. I am a woman-to-be who has lots to say. I choose not to speak. I choose not to speak because then you will have to focus on my face. I choose not to speak because I don't like how when I speak, my cheeks are round and stick out. I choose not to speak because my eyes are not pretty enough to distract you from the rest of my face. I choose not to speak because then you will have to look at me and then you will see my belly, eventually.

"No, Uncle, I am not a monk. I am just shy."

And fat.

THAT FATNESS, THOSE THICK SHOULDERS AND THE ROUND BELLY, wide thighs and full cheeks, have evolved in form; they have reduced in some spots and blossomed in others, especially after three children. I can fill a pencil skirt in many directions; this is a fact. I can wear a sari well, almost like a glove (or sometimes like a walking sausage), despite the rolls of midsection being exposed.

I have accepted my body.

And what else I have accepted is that people, from all walks of life, have always felt and still feel compelled to comment on and observe my body.

At the spa: "So all that callus on your feet is quite bad. I see that in a lot of women who carry extra weight around."

At the jewellery store: "For women with short, stubby fingers like you, it is probably better to go with a big ring, you know, to hide your finger fat."

At the dermatologist's office: "You wear a lot of makeup, huh? So people can focus on your face and not your heavy-set body?"

In the hallways at work: "You are so big in your pregnancy. It makes me uncomfortable just looking at you. Are you sure you should be wearing heels?"

A crush: "Well, I could consider going out with an Indian girl like you. I don't mind thick thighs, actually."

At the plastic surgeon's office: "Oh, that white deposit on your eyelid? Well that, my dear, is the result of too much eating. You have cholesterol built up; that's what that is. And looking at you, darling, it might be time to start drinking skim milk."

At a dinner party with my parents' friends: "You know, once women have kids, their bodies never get back to normal. I would watch yourself, Beti; otherwise you will turn out like your mother."

At the coffee shop: "Are you pregnant already? Gosh, you didn't have much time to get back into shape after your last one, did you? Well, people probably won't notice anything for a long time anyway, you know, because of your size."

In the airplane: "Are you sure you have your seat belt on? If you prefer, I can get you an extender."

Initially, I would rebut, or at least try: Well, I wear heels a lot, so maybe the callus is from that. I like big and bold jewellery anyway. I am sorry my growing uterus is making you uncomfortable. You can stick with your skinny white girlfriend, thank you very much. Skim milk it is, Doc! I would love to be one-eighth of my mother. Nope, not pregnant, just obese. Belted and ready, nothing to hide here.

And sure, at the all-you-can-eat breakfast, I see others looking at my plate. Of course, at the gym, I notice others seeing my struggle on the bike.

Okay, fine, in pictures, I might hide behind one of my children to cover my torso.

BARBRA STREISAND MAY NOT BE PLAYING IN THE BACKGROUND often these days. My playlist is more like Missy Elliott, the Cranberries, Malkit Singh and Drake, but I am not putting down my hairbrush. Barbra Streisand or bust!

I am no longer letting the unfiltered comments and audible gasps have a voice. I simply choose not to listen to the comments anymore. I hear them, I know they are being projected toward me, but I am not listening. I am listening to me. I no longer choose not to talk. I am no longer silent.

I am open with my entourage of family, friends, students, colleagues and neighbours. You have inquired about my BMI—no worries. I can feed that curiosity.

I have rolls because I bore children. I had three healthy pregnancies.

This scar on my thick thigh is from my hip replacement. I am grateful to the size of my thigh as I went through vigorous physiotherapy.

Yes, this callus is from the love of my stilettos! Nothing to hide here; I require some self-care pedicures every so often.

This is my truth. This is my body. I am not silent. I don't need your flowers anymore, Neil. My body garden is growing her own.

LOVING THE BIGGER FAT

Cate Root

---

*"But no one in my immediate family has been fat the way I was fat. ...
So fat that you'll always be fat, unless God or magic is involved."*

I WAKE UP TO THE CLATTER OF METAL HITTING HARDWOOD AND A thump. Next to me, my boyfriend is on the floor. Our woven-metal platform bed has partially collapsed. My side of the mattress remains on its perch, but the other half makes a lean-to against the floor. Broken bits of metal peek out from the mess underneath Alex. A deep moan rises from his belly and grows into a wail.

"Come on," I say. "Let's get up."

I stand and wait for him to join me. He's coming from a lower depth, and he moves slower than I do. "Come here." I hold open my arms. He falls into them and cries. "It's okay," I tell him. "It's okay."

We pull the mattress off the mangled frame. We bought this "Better Than a Box Spring" about ten months ago, one of many bed-related purchases since we've been together. It takes a lot to support us.

When we first met, Alex weighed about 500 pounds to my 215. Since then, we've made and lost more progress than I can comprehend—gaining, losing and regaining in the neighbourhood of 50 pounds. We have a way to go.

I'M STUCK IN TRAFFIC, TRYING TO KEEP MY PATIENCE. I LOOK AT my hands. Alex calls them doll hands. I don't understand what that means, though. My veins glow greenish against pink and white skin, which is otherwise marked by freckles and cat scratches. My nails are clipped short, unpainted, usually a little dirty. I think of a doll hand—consistently coloured, polished, its fingers splayed only for definition, never to grasp or touch.

Bored, I imagine how I must look to passing drivers. I see myself with a scarf on my head, fabulous vintage clothes, big sunglasses, driving a shiny boat of a car. I'm Janet Leigh from *Psycho*.

Then, of course, I realize that I'm not. The interior of my decade-old Chevy was already stained and cigarette-burned when I bought it. The exterior has a few dents and scratches and is always liberally dusted with pollen, leaves, burrs, dead flowers and bird shit. And, well, I'm me. I'm plain and tall. I wear glasses. I'm fat and red-headed. When I wake up in the morning, I look through a tossed-over room for the cleanest shirt to wear with my black pants. I skip makeup. I skip glamour.

And yet, in my mind's eye, I'm glamorous. Leigh is just an avatar, and an infrequent one at that. Most of the minor actors I cast to play Cate Root in my head are at least based on some version of me— green eyes, red hair, curls and curves.

But they're all stand-ins, waiting for the "true me" to emerge. Someday, I tell myself. Someday, I will be the right weight. Someday, when I'm closer to 200 pounds than 300, I'll just cast myself.

I feel like I've already been so many people. There's me, nine years old in a B-cup bra and taller than most of the boys in my class. Me at thirteen, fidgeting in a swimsuit, already self-conscious about stretch marks, a red web that quickly formed between my pale breasts and freckled shoulders. Me at fifteen, shrouded in an oversized flannel shirt.[1] Me at seventeen, trying on a new personality in New York City, hoping all the black would be slimming. Me at twenty-five, feeling graceful and lithe at 215 pounds, slipping on a pair of size 14 jeans and partying on a French Quarter balcony until dawn. Me now, twenty-eight and noticing every backache, every exacerbated hangover, every extra second it takes to push myself out of a low chair.

Those younger girls all feel lost to me now. I wonder, is it my fault? Was I supposed to take hold of them and keep them closer to me? Why can't I remember when I first got fat? Why can't I figure out what I looked like, really looked like, at any point in time? Why do old pictures always surprise me?

My family is big on pictures, but not their organizational trappings—photo albums, scrapbooks, anything tangible that can tell you a story about the past. We have photographs, but they're stuffed in drawers and set between the pages of novels. Some are even put into frames, but usually there are a handful of photos behind the one you can see. My parents have been married for thirty-five years, and their wedding photos consist of a bunch of blurry Polaroids stuck in a paper bag.

When I was in high school, I remember finding an old photo that shocked me. In it, I was probably seven or eight years old. I wore

---

1. The flannel was a style I picked up from a boy I liked years before. We carpooled to our K–12 school together. When I—an awkward, fat seventh grader—developed a crush on the high school junior, he stopped speaking to me. I grew to despise passing him in the halls, worrying so much about whether he'd make a face, say something rude or just ignore me. I remember how quickly his message reached me: *You are unattractive, and fat, and ugly, and wrong.* You are so wrong that your desire has the ability to upset a sixteen-year-old's social standing. He must save his reputation from your damning influence. And yet, in my own sophomore year, there I was in that same flannel.

denim play clothes and rode a carousel. My arms stretched above my head, and I grinned at the camera. Looking at it, I recognized the exuberance, but not the girl. That photograph made me question my entire history, the underlying assumption that I always was, am and will be fat, because the girl in that photo is exactly height-weight proportional. She's practically skinny.

I MET ALEX IN A MURDERER'S COURTYARD ON THE OUTSKIRTS OF the French Quarter in April 2008, when we both attended a garden party hosted by one of his co-workers, Patrick.

Romance was not in the air, even without the pernicious atmosphere of bleached-out gore.[2] By midnight most of the party guests had gone. Patrick, Alex, another guest and I were the only ones still sitting under the moonlight. Our conversation grew silly, talking about Patrick's childhood tours of Prince Edward Island and his family's obsession with *Anne of Green Gables*. At one point, we broke out in laughter, and Alex fell backward, taking the chair down with him. I laughed even harder but hoped my mirth wouldn't be construed as cruelty. My heart went out to Alex in his embarrassment, but then again, fat people falling down are pretty funny.

Alex didn't hit on me that night. By the time we were both available, about six months later, I'd convinced myself it was a bad idea. I'd spent my summer with a Jerk, and I wasn't ready to move on.

The summer I spent with the Jerk, at twenty-four and 215 pounds, I felt like I was on the verge of something. The Jerk was very attractive,

---

2. Most of the guests (including Alex) avoided the actual apartment, but I couldn't help my curiosity. The bathtub had been painted black—before the murder, Patrick said, although he couldn't be sure. The landlord tried to strip the paint, but there was no getting back to porcelain white. The tub, streaked with pitch black, stayed ashy grey.

and part of me thought being associated with him made me more attractive. This thing I was on the verge of—it was something more than popularity or validation. It was the idea that maybe, when people looked at me, I wouldn't be fat anymore. They would see me next to a man, six feet tall, well muscled, the type whose attractiveness couldn't be questioned—and I would fit.

Maybe I was a bit larger than they thought appropriate, but still, appealing. They would know there had to be something there. I would be beautiful, whole.

As late fall turned to winter, Alex and I began spending more time together. One night, under the charm of many drinks and quick-witted conversation, I took him home with me, even though I didn't want to pursue a romantic relationship. That decision was colossally misguided. Alex and I spoke every day; he was becoming one of my best friends. But I couldn't commit to him. I had to shut him down.

Somewhere in my black heart, I questioned my own motives. When things went south with the Jerk, I had found comfort in cardboard-box pizza and ice cream. I had already gained back fifteen or twenty pounds. I feared that if I got together with Alex, more would follow. If being with the attractive Jerk made me more attractive, would being with Alex make me fatter?

On our occasional short walks through the Quarter, Alex grew sweaty and began to pant. He couldn't keep up with me. And so one afternoon in December, staring out at the Mississippi River, I told Alex that I couldn't be with him. I just wasn't ready. I was afraid of getting hurt again. And I couldn't deal with the fact that he was really, really fat.

MOST OF MY FAMILY BATTLES WITH WEIGHT, BUT FEW ARE actually fat. Mostly, we're big—the women around five foot seven, the men around six feet. The women are what fashion magazines call "pear-shaped," holding all their weight around their hips and bellies, swollen like upright eggs. The men are large but rarely hulking. Their struggles come in beer bellies and double chins.

Over the years, my mother, father, sister, brother, aunts, uncles and grandmothers waxed and waned in their sizes. I remember their faces growing pudgier or thinner, and that my hugging arms couldn't always reach around someone's midsection. I have no memories of what made people get fat, giant bowls of cheese dip or faces smeared with chocolate cake. Life alone seemed to be fattening: ice cream in the summer, beers on the porch, cheese and crackers on the kitchen counter while Mom and Dad made dinner. What made people thin? Running ten miles a day. A diet of chicken and green vegetables with twice-a-day workouts. Mixing canned tuna with mustard and eating it off a Wasa cracker (I imagine that the cliché "This tastes like cardboard" was born the first time an English-speaker tasted the Scandinavian crisp breads).

You would think that this family history would foster commiseration and compassion. In reality, I resented the hell out of all of them. My mother's "fat" was a size 14—my "thin." My father's "struggle with weight," as far as I could tell, seemed to consist of a pudgy grade eight year, before he became a runner. My brother and sister have been overweight, pudgy, a little thick, at times.

But no one in my immediate family has been fat the way I was fat. Fat like 330 pounds fat. Fat like you can't reach to clean yourself properly in the shower. Fat like you're winded going up one flight of stairs. Fat like you have to eye each piece of furniture suspiciously, standing for hours at social occasions to avoid the humiliation of breaking a cheap chair. Fat like your joints hurt at the end of the day, every day. Fat like you feel you're always standing in the way. Fat like you just take up too much space in the world. So fat that you convince yourself that there's no other way. So fat that you'll always be fat, unless God or magic is involved.

And when we started dating, that's where Alex was. So fat that his mattress had a cavern down the centre. After a few nights of sliding into one another, we had to replace it. The second was no better, leaving us with backaches and joint pain. We switched to my mattress. Within a few months, the box spring broke. We bought a new bed frame. Within a year, it broke. Now we sleep on a mattress that rests on the floor. That there's nothing more to break should give me comfort. It doesn't.

THE HANDFUL OF MEN I SLEPT WITH BEFORE ALEX WERE WELL-muscled, hard frames. I loved the way it felt when they held me, almost like furniture. I loved that they were like walls or coat racks that I could hang on. Even as they pulled at my body, they felt solid and separate, an alien thing I could choose to let inside me. I marvelled at these men's bodies as if they were machines.

But Alex, Alex is soft. He is a mass of hot energy aching to be touched. He moans easily, moans when I kiss deep. Even in his sleep, he arches toward my fingers. He is responsive and enthusiastic. Our sex life is outside the rest of my experience—incomparable, private.

When we first got together, I imagined him as a great bear sprawled on the bed, and I scampered from one corner to the other, like a forest nymph, some playful, dainty thing. His solidity is different from that of the others. It's not that he's capable of lifting me or twisting me into positions; it's not his ability to manipulate my body or to handle my weight. It's that he makes me feel weightless.

ALEX AND I HAVE BEEN SHARING AN APARTMENT FOR ALMOST three years. He is my first boyfriend and the only man I've ever lived with. What strikes me is how completely unglamorous relationships actually are, how all of my emotions are wrapped up in something so minute and mundane. On a typical Tuesday night, I come home at nine and find Alex in the front room, folding laundry and watching cartoons. Mushroom soup (only four Weight Watchers points per serving!) simmers on the stove. Books, purses, sunglasses, papers, oranges and onions litter the kitchen table. Spices are left on the counter, the cabinet doors ajar. The light above the microwave is on—why does he always leave that light on? As I sit on the couch, Alex says, "Did you see the bedroom? I cleaned." Gratitude smothers my frustration.

Almost a year after I seduced and rejected Alex, he took me back. What changed in the interim? I realized that I was in love with him. I loved his stupid jokes,[3] his encyclopedic knowledge of language and trivia, his grasp on geography and world history and his jocular, casual acceptance of almost any feeling I share.

It's never glamorous. He bumps into the shelves in our narrow kitchen and breaks the dishes. The box springs collapse, and our bed frames splinter. Sometimes his pants rip. We overeat ice cream. I get angry because my pants are too tight. I worry about our future, our finances and our fitness. I worry deeply about our health. Alex tells me that he'll never leave me. I don't want to say, "There are other ways besides a breakup."

One year after the breaking of the bed frame, on a restless night, Alex comes to bed. There's a crack as he enters the room, adjusting the fan. I awake from my position on our new king mattress and box spring, only about a month old. We bought a bed frame, too, black, three-beam, labelled heavy-duty. It warped beyond usability within a few weeks. I meant to return it, to call it defective, but I missed

---

3. "Well, you know what they say," Alex prompts. When someone, usually not me, indulges him with a response, he mixes two aphorisms, like "A bird in the hand gathers no moss." Somehow, I just know he's been telling that joke since he was twelve years old.

the window. It leans against the wall in the corner, waiting to be thrown out.

I'm upset. Alex asks why, and I can't tell him. I think about his three pieces of toast at breakfast, his two sandwiches for lunch or his decision to eat a quesadilla when I want taco salad for dinner. It takes effort to not audibly police his food intake, even though I know that tactic doesn't work. I think about my mom admonishing me for eating too many oranges, my dad eyeing my third piece of bread, my brother nibbling on a handful of almonds while the rest of the family demolishes a spread of cheese and crackers.

This is a choice, I remind myself. Loving Alex is a choice. Loving myself, fat and all, is a choice. It is minute and mundane, a series of efforts and setbacks and some truly excellent progress. Still, we have a way to go.

REFLECTIONS

Sally Quon

"Do you know what it's like to live in a lake town and go to the beach at six in the morning because there isn't anyone else there at that time?"

I LIVE IN A HOUSE OF MIRRORS. NOT BY CHOICE—THE CONDO I rent just happened to be decorated that way. At first, I found it unnerving. I simply wasn't used to seeing my reflection. Then I found it annoying. Who the hell thought it would be a good idea to put mirrors on the wall behind the stove? But eventually, like all things we are faced with every day, I just stopped noticing.

Even though I'm surrounded by mirrors, I seldom look at them. I don't like the way I look. I am fat. Not your garden-variety "I could stand to lose twenty pounds" fat. I'm what's referred to as morbidly obese, tipping the scales at three-hundred-plus pounds.

The funny thing is, unless you actually look at a mirror, it's fairly easy to deceive yourself. The image you have of yourself is seldom anything like what your real physical appearance is. Often, when I do happen to see myself in a mirror, I'm surprised to see just how heavy I am. I'll stop and look. I'll wonder if I've lost any weight. I'll wonder if this shirt that I'm wearing is effectively covering my bulges. I'll think, "It's not that bad. There are plenty of people heavier than I am." It's a coping mechanism: rationalization.

I work as a caregiver for seniors who wish to remain in their own homes. Being a "person of volume" has its drawbacks in this industry.

I've had clients refuse my service because I'm too fat. I make them uncomfortable. One client who doesn't think my weight is an issue has a second bedroom with mirrors on the closet doors. As I am there for an overnight shift, although I don't sleep, the second bedroom is where I spend my time. But there is something wrong with his mirrors. In his mirrors, I am a whale. I am a Buddha. I am the fat lady from the circus posters. I don't know if it's because I'm sitting on the bed or if he just has faulty mirrors, but there's no way I look like that.

Except I do.

I just don't understand it. I don't eat fast food or junk food. I try to eat regular meals in normal portions. I don't do desserts and I don't binge eat. I try to get exercise, in spite of my limited mobility. And even though my mirrors at home are encouraging, this one tells an entirely different story.

With morbid fascination, I can't help looking. If I were the circus fat lady, I'd have to charge myself admission. Where did all that blubber come from? I hate the way I look, and I hate the way that makes me feel. If I'm not thinking about it, I'm reasonably happy—but I can't help thinking about it.

Do you know what it's like to go to a restaurant and be shown to a booth you don't fit into? Do you know what it's like to have someone offer you dessert and, when you refuse, hear them say, "Oh, are you on a diet?" Or have everyone at a party watch you to see what you put on your plate?

Do you know what it's like to live in a lake town and go to the beach at six in the morning because there isn't anyone else there at that time?

Booths and bathing suits are not the only things I don't fit into: clothing, cars and—oh my God—public washroom stalls. Amusement parks are out of the question, and I have to lose at least twenty-five pounds if I want to try ziplining. Parking spaces. That's one you probably wouldn't have thought of. Life jackets. Absolutely anything that says "one size fits all." Of course, even when I was a normal size, I'd toss those. Underwear—I eventually just stopped wearing it.

But the thing that rankles me more than anything else? It's not other women with perfect bodies. No, it's men who think they're being cute when they say, "I can't. I have to watch my girlish figure."

Fuck off.

LEARNING TO LIVE, LARGE

Tracy Manrell

"I have lived my life in two genders. And, in both of them, fat."

I WAS ASSIGNED FEMALE AT BIRTH. AND, DESPITE IT NEVER FEEL-
ing right, I largely lived that assignment for forty-eight years. I was
a daughter, sister, granddaughter, niece, lesbian, wife and mama.
Most sweetly, a mama. In my forty-ninth year, I began the process
of change. By my fifty-second birthday, I was socially, hormonally
and legally male. A soft, queer, non-binary, transmasculine human
deeply connected to women, to women's issues and to my feminist
outlook on the world—with a beard.

I have lived my life in two genders. And, in both of them, fat.

MY RELATIONSHIP WITH MY BODY HAS ALWAYS BEEN COMPLI-
cated. My childhood body had a visceral reaction to dresses, girl toys,
the colour pink and other social constructs and behavioural expectations because it was perceived as being female. I was tall, and by age
eleven my feet were so large that adult-sized women's shoes didn't
fit me any longer. I was relieved and excited to "have to" buy boy's
shoes yet shamed by them, and my desire for them, at the same time.
I was athletic but far from "girl-sized." In grade three, my teacher
called me a bull elephant. I didn't know what that was, but I knew

it was bad. I knew I was bad. In the class photos, I'm always the one standing at the back with the biggest boys, right beside the teacher. Awkward, uncertain, anxious, sometimes angry and often feeling I didn't fit in. I recall wishing many times that I was small and could disappear, tucked among the little smiling girls down in front.

At puberty the real dysphoria began. The body I was assigned began to betray me in new ways. When I menstruated before any of my friends, the panic rose. I tried to hide my chest in oversized *Peanuts* cartoon sweatshirts. The teasing about my boyish presentation became so painful and shame-filled that I grew my hair. I pored over the Sears catalogue for clothes that were intended for girls yet didn't compromise my integrity and sense of self. Clothes that didn't require me to suppress the urge to rip them from my body, frantic with distress. I began to eat.

I ate when I was angry. I ate when I was sad. I ate to distract myself from reliving painful memories. I ate to avoid fears and worries. I ate for comfort. I ate to disconnect. I ate to calm my companions: loneliness and anxiety. I once stole money for food because my need to eat was greater than my shame for being a thief. I snuck food from our kitchen and hid it under my bed. I shoved candy wrappers down the furnace vents to hide my tracks and somehow didn't burn down the house. I repeatedly re-enacted a TV ad from the 1970s wherein a Viking grabs a chocolate bar from a treasure chest, shoves half of it into his mouth, swallows and shouts with a joy, strength and power I wished I had.

My body and my relationship with food have taken up a lot of physical and mental space for much of my life.

THE EBB AND FLOW OF A LIFE DISCONNECTED FROM A BODY CAN BE like treading water. You stay afloat but don't move from your position much. Your head is up, looking around, engaging. But below the neck things are otherworldly, slower moving, detached.

I recognize and am thankful that, despite the fractious relationship I have had with it, my given body has brought great joy to me and to others in my life. In that female body I grew up active—running in the wind, biking with a freedom that no other activity brought to me, swimming outside in the rain. In that body I worked my first jobs, volunteered in a hospital and excelled in team sports. I negotiated my way through and graduated from high school. My body has kept me going through depression and anxiety so deep that life sometimes didn't feel worth living. In that body I made my way through university. I supported my best friend as he died of AIDS. I launched my career, often wearing clothes that ate me alive, believing that my life success depended on them.

As I became fat, my body became more political, stirred the conservative pot within my family of origin and made me stronger. I came out as lesbian. I found deep, lasting love and committed myself to life with a woman who has made my heart sing for twenty-five years now. My hands were the first to touch our children as they entered the world. By design, the first words our children heard earthside were mine, welcoming them. My female body could comfort my wife and our children for years even when it often didn't—couldn't—comfort me.

And all along the sense that something was wrong and missing was ever present. I was getting older and didn't want to look back with regret. I was terrified and yet had to make a choice. Commit myself to being more present and accepting of the body I was assigned and the size it had become. Or allow the questions about who I really was to be spoken aloud and see where that took me.

MY FIRST INJECTION OF TESTOSTERONE BROUGHT EUPHORIA TO battle my long-standing dysphoria. I didn't expect that so quickly. But, then again, I wasn't sure what to expect, really. With each subsequent injection the joy grew, the questions and fears thinned and the noise in my head about the wrongness of my body started to quiet.

Unlike many cisgender boys in puberty, I was charmed by my cracking voice. In fact, it made me laugh more than once. My previously good singing voice became truly awful, and I'm still waiting to see if I ever get it back. The hair on my legs grew well in some spots but hardly at all in others. Knee bangs. I impatiently awaited my first chin hairs and within a year was relieved to be in the group that can grow a full beard. I'm lucky; it's not a guarantee. But the hair on my chest was among the best changes. It was these early, furry beginnings that allowed me to look at parts of my body with genuine wonderment and joy, perhaps for the first time. For the first time, I could see my true self.

When I had read about trans people "seeing themselves for the first time," I was always confused. Although I tended to resist looking at myself unless necessary, I knew what I looked like. Both my size and my femininity were always hard to see, but I knew what my body looked like. I was taken aback, then, when my beard began to grow and I caught a glimpse of a familiar, warm masculine person in the mirror one day. Not all me yet also as much me as I had ever been. For the first time, I wanted to look, and it was very emotional. I saw the gentle trans man, not the woman. I saw the beard, not the fat. I saw joy, freedom, and I felt I could fly.

I had always imagined myself as a big Grizzly Adams type with a dark, bushy and slightly wild beard, broad shoulders and a firm yet soft belly. The bigness of my female body was painful, shameful and ugly. But a soft, barrel-chested male version of me was a warm and kind, if private, thought. I imagined a red flannel shirt, Levi's, plaid boxers and wool socks. Ironic, really, as I had grown up with clean-shaven, disciplined men with military haircuts in suits with ties. I didn't relate to much in those men. They weren't approachable and they rarely showed emotion. They scared and intimidated me. This made the male presence inside of me terrifying. How could I be a man? I didn't want to be what I thought a man was. This added to my fear, shame and self-hate. But the truth that I was much more male than female was eating away at me, and I had to find peace.

Over time I began to see and trust that within me was a male presence unlike the men I had grown up watching. The male inside me questioned the existing definitions of masculinity. Inside me was the kind of soft, sensitive person I rarely saw in the masculinized world around me. And realizing I was a good, kind and clearly feminine man slowly made the process less scary.

AS MY BODY CHANGED, I BEGAN TO SEARCH OUT PEOPLE LIKE ME on social media. The need for affirmation and to "find our people" is universal. Although I always observed that life as a big man seemed different than life for big women, I was struck on a new level just how different these worlds are.

Women and men have different definitions of a fat body, I observe. Women are much harder on themselves. A woman sees herself as fat when carrying an extra ten or even five pounds. A man with those same extra pounds (and more) sees it as muscle or brawn on their bodies.

Big women talk about and fight for size acceptance, for their place at the table, battle messages that they are unattractive, unstable, unlovable, uncontrolled, unfuckable. They have to convince themselves that, despite the messaging in almost every corner of life, they have self-worth and their size does not define anything about them.

Many men, on the other hand, seem to perceive themselves as sexy and attractive at weights that distress women, both emotionally and socially. So universal is the messaging that boys and men have inherent value and sexual prowess, and are desirable to women, that most seem to grow up with these beliefs, size be damned. And women extend this same leeway to big men, too. In fact, I began to notice that an objectively "fat" man is referred to by men and women alike as a beast, a bear, brawny, burly, big boy, sexy daddy. Their size may be seen as a bonus, not a source of shame, rejection or self-hate as it often is for women.

This is a new world in which I am moving. And exploring it still leaves me puzzled and questioning myself at times. Am I able to see and experience joy in myself now because I am externally becoming the person I have always been inside? Is it because my body is finally aligning with my mind and heart? Or am I able to see and experience joy in myself because, despite my years of shouting just the opposite, I have internalized society's messages that big men are different—better—than big women? Can I tolerate my fat easier as a man because big bros are strong, sexy beasts? Will I find more peace with my size as a man than I ever could as a woman?

Don't get me wrong. I am a parent to a cisgender male and know he has his social and physical vulnerabilities, as do his male peers. But they are different. Very different. I have lived life in both genders, both as a fat person. For me, it is easier being a fat man than being a fat woman.

TWO YEARS INTO TRANSITION, I OBTAINED A REFERRAL TO A SURgeon who could permanently change the landscape of my chest. My brain needed my body to match its vision of who I am inside. I needed my external body to move in the world in one gender. I wanted fewer stares and whispers. I wanted to pass as male to experience the confidence and peace that might come with that. I needed the dignity of using men's rooms without worrying for my safety.

Getting this referral was not easy for someone of my size. It took nearly a year and the efforts of other big trans folk to break down the barriers of being fat and transgender and needing gender-affirming surgery. As many fat folks know, the medical system isn't set up to serve us. And it can be punitive and full of land mines.

Where I live, the magic to getting top surgery is BMI: body mass index. The magic BMI number is ideally thirty, but thirty-five might work if you find a flexible surgeon. My BMI was sixty. But one surgeon in my province had finally agreed to work with folks with BMIs over thirty-five. So I picked him and waited for my intake appointment. While I waited, I quite easily lost eleven pounds, excited about what was to come. When the day came, I paid out of pocket to travel to the surgeon's city because he doesn't work in mine. Being fat is expensive, too, sometimes.

On the boat ride to see him, my heart was soaring. I had never felt such joy in my big body in my life—ever. Yet when I arrived my hopes were dashed. He said that he had never done this surgery on someone my size. He had agreed to be flexible with BMI but he didn't intend to be *this* flexible. Familiar shame came rushing back. He and/or the anesthesiologist could deny me what I want—what I need—because I'm fat. They would discuss it—me, my fat and my acceptability—and let me know.

I plunged into a familiar depression that hung around for nearly two months. Instead of losing more weight to help address his concerns, I gained ten pounds back. I was in a dark hole for a long time, once again.

So far the surgeon has not refused me. I have a new list of weight-related things to worry about since we met, but he agreed to perform the surgery when my name reaches the top of his waiting list if I still want to do it. It's not a matter of choice, though. I need this surgery to be my full, physical self. So I requested to be on his waiting list, despite his reticence to have me there. At the time I'm writing this, six more months have passed and I'm still waiting. I called last week to ask how much longer and was reminded I'm complicated. It will take time—many more months. Be patient.

I'm scared and the wait makes it harder. My deep need for this surgery is tempered by my fears of being vulnerable to a medical system that scorns me for my size and my gender identity. Will I be treated equally as a fat person? Will I be respected? What about when I'm unconscious? If I'm in pain, will I have equal and fair access to medications to help me cope? Will I get the same care as someone with an "acceptable" BMI? Will I be shamed over and over by the providers I will inevitably meet through this process? Am I still waiting for a surgery date now because I'm fat and complicated?

AS I WAIT AND WORRY, I'M WORKING WITH A WONDERFUL PHYSician who specializes in obesity medicine. I am aware of my great luck to have found her. She has a team of committed, politically aware, sensitive and intelligent women working in her office. She has gone to bat for me both as a person of size and as a trans person more than once within the medical community. She is committed to helping me meet my goals, which, for now, include losing weight to have the most successful gender-affirming chest surgery I can.

She fought for me to get accepted for surgery with my exaggerated BMI. In fact, she dug until she got my preferred surgeon's private cellphone number, then phoned him to talk about body mass indexes as outdated tools for assessing a patient's suitability for surgery. She's a warrior in a field that is poorly understood by most and dismissed as invalid or unworthy by many. She is an ally for obese patients who are often disrespected or disbelieved by health-care professionals. She's my kind of person.

But she and I both know that the surgeon is right to some degree: I will get the best surgical results and recover with the least pain and potential complications if I can shed some weight.

I rarely feel terribly optimistic about my ability to lose and keep off weight. And I don't feel that much different this time. But at least now I have a team joining me in the ring. It's not just me, alone against the world of food and my magnetic attraction to it.

But she hates the word *fat*. She sees only one use for it: insult. It's a word she feels people, particularly women, use to degrade themselves and each other. It's a word people use to attack, hurt or belittle. The first time I used it in her presence she stopped me short. That word is not allowed in her office. Ever. She sees it as disrespectful to her practice and to every patient she supports.

Maybe it's my queer identity that makes her opinion of the word *fat* the one thing we disagree on. The queer community is famous for reclaiming words that have historically been used against us: queer, dyke, fag, tranny. Used by the right people and in the right context, these words carry their own positive power. And they are just words—adjectives, descriptors. Frankly, there was a long time when if someone called me a fat dyke, I could say, Yes. Yes, I am. Fat and (for now) a dyke. What's your point?

So when I call myself fat, I am not putting myself down. I am fat. I wear glasses. I have brown hair and a brown beard. I am transgender. And none of this is inherently bad.

ENCIRCLED

Jen Arbo

"In life outside the dojo ... I am expected to feel shame about the shape I am, a pang of regret for the shape that could have been."

AS I ENTER MY LATE FORTIES, MY TORSO, BREASTS AND UPPER arms are slithering down my frame and forming an egg around my middle. When I see myself in building glass reflections and mirrored elevators, I have half-hearted internal conversations about my aging, soft body. They're usually focused on how to keep my pants where they belong as the downward ooze of skin and fat necessitates increasingly larger-waisted pants, and yet the jelly, amorphous state of my postpartum innards means the pants sag no matter how crisply laundered they are.

I wonder if I should start wearing belts, I think. Would a belt affix my bits to the right height and make me look slimmer or feel better about myself?

I feel quite good about the shape I inhabit, for the most part. I'm happy about the life I've lived that's brought me here, to this size and shape, the child I carried and love with my whole heart, the spouse I share adventures with. I am loved—by myself and by others. I don't define the space I physically occupy based on the approval of the people I occupy it with, whether they are strangers, friends or children.

I do see the judgment of people, though, their faces neon billboards as my 215-pound, five-foot shape navigates between tables set too close together at a crowded restaurant or stops to take a drink of water while out hiking. The judgment is always adjacent to food or fitness. They observe me as if I were a headless body and then flash to my detached face to study whether I'm aware of the space the body occupies. But the thing is, I don't actually care. I am loved—by myself and by others.

The judgers never want to make eye contact, but I enjoy finding their eyes and holding their gaze a bit too intensely, a cobra being charmed by the hypnotic sound of the pungi. If one of us is going to be uncomfortable and be made to squirm, it shouldn't be me for merely existing.

I avoid media that have decided I am too heavy or too fat or too round. I don't follow celebrity news or modern fashion magazines, consciously choosing to bypass the toxic venom that tells me I'm not good enough. For years I subscribed to a magazine about simple living, but it morphed slowly through different editors and ownership to be about simple clothes, and then simple cooking, and then, ever so slowly, simple diets.

Unsubscribe.

MY DOCTOR HAS HINTED I SHOULD LOSE SOME WEIGHT—"JUST FOR general health, you know"—but, when pressed, she can't tell me how much I should try to shave off or what health challenge I'm trying to avoid. My labs are clear, my skin is happy, I move my body every day in some form or another. I went to a gym for a while to make myself stronger, got bored and quit, but I didn't feel the regret for stopping that I expected.

When I was pregnant with my son I felt larger than the world, and anything across my stomach made me nauseous. After I had recovered from the physical trauma of his birth and was working on becoming a Functioning Adult Human again, I tricked myself into thinking I once again liked belts. I was convinced they would hide the unfamiliar c-section scar and stretched-out flabby skin skirt I didn't know how to dress. I bought ridiculously tall elastic belts—basically, corsets—with adjustable buckles and bound myself into them. They hurt and bit into my sides.

But my son presented the ultimate challenge: how to raise a son and teach him that shape doesn't matter, without caring about my own?

"Mama, I love your soft, squishy belly," he would say as he awkwardly patted me with his damp toddler hand, fingers outstretched. He would snuggle into me and we fit so perfectly together. Love told me this is the shape I was meant to be.

I AM CAREFUL ABOUT HOW I REFER TO MY BODY. I AM NOT A PEAR or an apple; I am not a piece of fruit with legs. I don't say I am "plus-sized" unless the person I am speaking with won't otherwise understand me. I don't often say "fat" because when I say it, it feels like I'm spitting out the word. I am short and I am wide. I am Jack Sprat's nameless wife.

It is challenging to clothe a short and wide person. I've learned the clothes that fit me best usually don't hang from hangers in the store. They are hard to display and often cost more. Modern retail fashion has shuffled the "speciality sizes" into expensive boutiques or online only, and so I've figured out what sites ship the fastest and have the most generous and easiest return policies. When I find a shirt or pants that fit me well, I buy all the colours I like.

But belts—belts make me question my own confidence. I put one on every once in a while and it folds and tugs at my stomach, the buckle uncomfortably digging into my navel, and leaves imprints on my skin: patterned, red scales. Belts ruin my T-shirts and add bulk around my middle like a shelf upon which I can rest disappointment.

Belts make me care what shape I inhabit because they dangle a promise of being able to reframe my frame. They force my feelings up into my throat, where I choke on them, and shove my sloppy belly down. Belts are always too tight, too heavy, too skinny, too small, too oppressive. I am pushed into places I do not wish to inhabit. In those mirrors on empty elevators on my way to the fourth floor, belts are optimistic boa constrictors on large prey, slowly crushing me to death.

I admit I own a few belts. One is a bright orange, elastic baseball-uniform belt I got from the men's section of the local thrift shop. It has a leather tongue with punch holes, a length adjuster on the elastic and a brass buckle with fang-like double prongs. It is two inches of sturdy, secure elastic with only a bright white "Rawlings" scrolled on the loop to give away that it belongs on a pair of polyester breeches. I like its cheerful brightness. I like that the fabric feels okay on my tag-abhorrent skin. Mostly, I like that I can stand to wear it long enough that people will leave me alone about needing a goddamned belt to look better. It is camouflage I wear to blend in.

We cannot talk about belts without talking about belt loops. Pants manufacturers seem to have settled on an efficient five loops: two at the closure, one on each hip and one at the back. Five belt loops mean my belt shifts and moves and pops above the pants. I say six is a better number: two at the closure, one on each hip and one on the top of each butt cheek, spaced apart. Heck, add a seventh in there, too, in the middle. Belts and how we attach them are why plus-sized clothing is so often elastic-waisted. "The belt's built right in!" they exclaim. "No embarrassing wardrobe malfunctions due to your badly shaped body existing!"

A SIMPLIFIED AND SHORT HISTORY OF BELTS: ALTHOUGH WORN IN the Bronze Age as a place to hang weapons, belts were popularized in modern fashion in the 1920s as waistlines lowered on men's trousers, serving a largely decorative function. Today, we have people who are convinced they are essential clothing, and we don't know how to back out of what belts have become.

WHEN DID I STOP LOVING BELTS? ELEVEN-YEAR-OLD ME LOVED A useful belt. If you were an all-in Girl Guide like I was, you wore that one-inch, elastic utility belt with pride and hooked your pencil, pouch and whistle-on-a-lanyard to it. It was a place to hold important things and let you be hands-free without the frilliness of a hand-bag or the bulk of a backpack. You could put maps in your pouch, or a compass, or perhaps a bit of trail mix to keep you going. That belt helped me more equitably navigate the world made for men and boys, a Bronze Age warrior free to hold her spear aloft and impale the bastards who stood in her way.

As I grew hips and breasts, I started needing to have all my pants tailored with darts, modified waists and shortened hems, and I had to start shopping in the "curvy juniors" section. Belts became oppres-sive instruments of cinching. Belts became a line drawn across the middle of me, accentuating curves I was told I shouldn't have or shouldn't like. Belts dictated what the right waist measurements were and made me feel that it was my job to fit into them, and not their job to wrap around me.

When I was sixteen, my mother gave me a fantastic belt that no longer fit her. "Here," she said. "It's too small for me, though I wish it wasn't. It's so ... flashy."

She was wistful. She had bought it for a costume party and just kept wearing it long after Cleopatra's wig was put away. It was the late eighties, and fashion was over the top. It was gold metal, flexible and shaped like a rope. It jingled when you walked and flashed in the sun. It was a serpent, with ruby eyes and a forked tongue, and a cunning latch that worked by shoving the tail of the snake into the mouth. In my mind, it was jewellery, not a belt. I wore it until it broke, and I cried—I actually cried—when it did.

Early-twenties me owned belts of many colours and styles: metal, leather, elastic, woven, plastic. I shed them all as soon as I was home. A fashion-focused friend told me that not wearing belts was telling. "You know, Jen," she sniffed. "They really show off how put together you are—not only how you dress and the outfit you picked out, but also as a person, really."

But I am put together, I would think. Aren't I?

YOU KNOW HOW YOU ASSOCIATE CERTAIN CATEGORIES OF CLOTHing with people in your life? A friend loves polka dots, especially tiny ones. Another wears dresses all year round. Yet another is known for pocket squares. My thing is glasses—I love them because they have nothing to do with my weight or the shape of my body. But you know what no one is ever known by? Belts. No one is ever known by the belts they wear.

Scene: funeral home, interior. A woman, red-eyed and grief-stricken, stands at a podium and faces the audience. "I don't know what I will do without my dear husband now that he is gone." She breaks down, sobbing. After a moment, she gathers herself and says: "But I take comfort knowing he's left behind his extensive belt collection, which is what I will think of forevermore when I think of Charles." End scene.

THERE IS BUT ONE MEANINGFUL BELT IN MY LIFE, A BELT THAT feels right: my blue belt. I've earned it after four years in the dojo, and I'm hoping to replace it with a brown and then a black belt in the coming years.

It took a long time for me to get up the courage to shyly ask about women's classes. I sat watching my son throw punches and kicks for two years before I did. And I had to tailor my *gi* to fit my hips and breasts.

But you know what fit perfectly right from the get-go?

The first belt I earned, and all the belts after that. It feels comforting around my waist. My blue belt is a symbol, not an accessory. Perhaps I'm too old or too stiff or too soft to be a karate practitioner, but I attend classes each week with a group of women of varying ages and sizes, and we have found a community together. No shame, only confidence. In life outside the dojo, however, I am expected to feel shame about the shape I am, a pang of regret for the shape that could have been.

When I don't feel the shame I'm told I should, I wonder if there is something wrong with my emotional intelligence or functionality. I have been told I can be too blunt, too capricious, too sardonic, too detached. I am always too something, never the right shape for the box held open to squash me into. I have been conditioned to feel shame about being a short and wide woman, but what do I do with the shame I feel for not feeling shame? The self-help and diet sections have plenty of books on how to shed the shame for fatness, but what of the shame for being okay with my shape? It is a vicious circle I cannot escape.

OUROBOROS IS THE SERPENT DEPICTED EATING ITS OWN TAIL IN ancient mythologies, and I guess also depicted in that jingly metal belt my mother gave me. Modern interpretations suggest Ouroboros was too large to be contained, and that the circular shape is a depiction of Ouroboros encircling the world as the only place that fits. It is easy to think that Ouroboros is eating its own tail to sustain life, consuming to be reborn and consumed again, a symbol of the cyclical nature of life and death, returning to the ground.

But my version is different. I imagine that Ouroboros felt such great shame for her shape. Can you imagine being deemed too large for the world? I imagine she chose to encircle the world—a belt of sorts—to teach those who deemed her too large the miserable lesson they deserved. I don't believe she is eating her tail to sustain her life. She is holding her tail in her mouth as she constricts around them, a warrior free to smother the bastards who stood in her way and told her she should not be as happy as she was.

"I will become that which binds me," she hissed.

THE TOXIC FAT TRAIN

Lynne Jones

---

*"Would they say they love me exactly as I am and then
suggest we join a gym or start preparing salads?"*

"HEY, BABE, THE NEW DEF LEPPARD ALBUM IS HERE! I'LL GET IT,
and we can go back to mine and listen to it."

My head felt like a helium balloon as I sashayed across the record shop to join him. My new leather boots squeaked on the laminate
floor, and we both chuckled. I tried to ignore the recently hatched
butterflies that seemed to have formed a mosh pit in my belly.

He'd called me "babe."

"Okay, cool, I hope it's as good as their last one. It's taken them
long enough!"

Look at me, I thought, so nonchalant. You'd swear I wasn't a nov-
ice at this. Ritchie was my first boyfriend. We'd had one date and one
kiss, but at fourteen that was pretty serious.

He gave me a killer smile, and the dimple on his left cheek made
an appearance. I'm almost certain I swooned for a split second.

His fingers flicked adeptly through the rows of alphabetized
albums, stopping only to push back loose strands of his extremely
long hair from his face. It was the late eighties—"hair metal" was
big, and it was our shared obsession of music that had brought us
together. He picked up an old Whitesnake record and began studying
it, totally lost in his passion while I tried to control mine.

I caught a glimpse of myself in the mirror. Being a girlfriend suited me, I decided. I felt good; my jeans were extra tight, clinging to every shapely arc of my developing body, and my prized boots were big, chunky Doc Martens. I had nagged my mum for months to get me a pair. The pretty dresses she used to make me wear when I was too young to protest were long gone, and now my adolescent uniform was a battered old leather jacket, too-tight jeans and a band T-shirt.

I had never been interested in boys; I was content with exploring my teenage life with my friends. I was curvier than most of the girls in my school year but I never really thought about it. I was comfortable in my skin; I walked everywhere, and I played hockey and netball for the school teams. I had loads of friends and easygoing parents. I was living the teenage dream. When Ritchie moved from another village after his parents divorced, his hair, love of rock music and charisma meant he quickly became part of our group of friends.

"Hey, gorgeous," were his first-ever words to me. After weeks of my being oblivious to his obvious flirting, my friends took me aside and told me he liked me. Very shortly after, he asked me to be his girlfriend. I didn't even think about whether I liked him or not: he wanted me, and I couldn't resist the attention.

My face became a flush of red every time he talked to me. Our first kiss was messy and wet, and I wondered what the fuss was about, but he wanted to be with me. I had a new feeling of lightness, of slight permanent nausea, a gentle lurch of my belly every time he reached for my hand. I had barely stopped smiling since we'd become an "item."

The Def Leppard album was set aside on the rack, and he continued to flick through the records. He picked out the latest album of an American all-female band. I had been learning to play the guitar for a couple of years, and I was utterly obsessed; I was certain I'd be in an all-girl rock band one day. I wanted to be a part of the change in the sexist music industry; I had feminist ideas from a young age.

Ah, he knows me so well, I thought.

He pointed at the cover, and I glanced momentarily into my hero's deep blue eyes. Could he be more perfect? I pondered in my smitten, love-sickened mind. He stared at me, a long smouldering linger across my teenage body. The hair pricked at the back of my neck. I felt like I was vulnerable prey about to be devoured; I didn't dislike it. He looked back at the record cover in his hand.

"Why can't you look like them? If you lost a few pounds, maybe you could wear sexier things like they do."

His words flew swiftly and bitterly through me like a pesticide plane and systematically wiped out the population of butterflies inside me. They were replaced by a lead brick that hooked from my fixed smile to deep inside my puppy fat–coated belly. It was a comment that would be the death of my first relationship and the birth of my self-esteem issues.

It was the first time someone had made a cruel comment to me about my weight, but it was certainly not the last. It was the catalyst for my descent into self-loathing and the feeling of inadequacy created by my constant comparisons to slimmer and (I started to believe) prettier girls. I stopped playing sports in school, went out less and started wearing baggy jumpers to hide my flab. I dyed my hair brightly to take the emphasis off my body. I became like a chameleon, morphing to fit in with any boy who showed an interest. I found myself having relationships with people who valued me as little as I valued myself; I avoided relationships with good, genuine men because I never believed I truly deserved them. I had casual encounters because that's all I thought I was worth. I pretended it was all I wanted—not caring made the inevitable rejection easier.

Over the years, the comments came thick and fast: If you lost some weight, you'd be so pretty. I love you exactly as you are, but don't put on any more weight. Why can't you look more like your skinny blond friend? You go to the gym? Really? What happened?

I'd date you if you lost thirty pounds. Wow, you've got a flabby belly, I had no idea. You dress well to hide it.

With each failed relationship, my self-esteem plummeted, my chocolate consumption increased, and I went from curvy to lumpy. I felt grateful for any attention, validation that I wasn't some hideous Jabba the Hutt figure. The unpleasant liaisons with inappropriate men further fuelled my lack of self-love, and I had learned to accept the comments about my size. I believed it was what I deserved for being such a failure at dieting, at life.

I tried everything. I tried to feed my emptiness with fruit and vegetables, but my broken heart wanted comfort. Lettuce didn't fill the void. By my mid-thirties I seemed to have been in and out of relationships and casual flings forever, and I was no happier for it. I decided to take some time out.

I started spending more time with my friends. One night of drunken abandonment ended in us signing up to an online dating site and deciding to rate all the less attractive guys as "super hot" and the really good-looking ones as "average." Our aim was to increase the self-esteem of the less attractive ones. Of course, we were not entirely invisible despite our vodka-fuelled imaginary invisibility cloak. I woke the next morning with a stinking hangover and a bad belly from laughing so much. I also had an inbox full of messages from a man in a kilt with a guitar hanging around his very broad chest. The conversation I had been having with him the night before via email was a blur, and I cringed reading back over my drunken rantings. I sent him a polite message thanking him for his interest, but I was not looking for anything.

He pursued me relentlessly. Somehow, within a few days, I was standing in my kitchen waiting for my knight in shining armour to turn up for our first date. He arrived in a battered old Ford. I kept checking myself in the mirror. I wished I had told him I was fat. I imagined him turning up and leaving immediately because of my hideousness. He walked in and gave me a massive bear hug.

"Your photo doesn't do you justice; you're far more beautiful in real life."

I let out my breath. We quickly became a couple. He showered me with gifts and compliments and made me feel like I was worth something. He told me he loved me and I was beautiful through and through, that my curves excited him.

"Something to grab on to," he would say.

I would often turn and catch him staring lovingly at me. I told him how much I hated my body. I let down my guard and talked openly for the first time in my life about past experiences, mistakes and how I longed to accept my flesh or miraculously lose a load of weight overnight.

"How can you not see what I see? You are stunning, a goddess. One day you'll see it for yourself."

I felt I'd struck gold, and I went along with it, enjoying the adulation. We moved in together after a few months. He would bring home family-sized bars of chocolate and take-aways and then complain that he was getting fat, but he loved me more the bigger I got. He stopped eating the junk but kept bringing it home. I kept gorging; the comfort was new, this feeling of loved up-ness and not having to deny my chocolate need. I felt free. He loved me just the way I was.

Although I became more comfortable with my body, once the madness of the first few months of living together passed, something was never quite right. I never really "felt it." Love. With him. Sex felt obligatory; the passion felt forced, fake, and I think sometimes he sensed it.

"You just don't get it; we were made for each other. This is deeper than love," he said. He would stroke my hand, and I longed to feel that deep connection with him. I wanted nothing more than to be able to spend hours lost in conversation with him, needing nothing more than me, him and the space of silence and companionship, but I didn't feel on the same page as him.

I blamed myself once again: Was I pushing away a good guy again because I loathed myself so much? I was bigger than I had ever been, past the point of even being able to cover my lumps with baggy clothes. I retreated from social events; I was happy to stay at home and watch television with a pizza.

"Everything I've ever wanted is here, with you," he would say as we cuddled on the sofa.

He asked me to marry him several times; I eventually agreed. It still didn't feel right, but I had made my decision and felt I should consider myself lucky that someone loved me as he did. He lost his job shortly after we got engaged. For nearly a year I increased my workload, brought in money to keep us both. He'd complain about how much he hated his life, and he had no clothes or couldn't afford nice things. I would buy them for him to stop his moods. He'd complain about how I didn't like sex: Was it because I didn't want a man who didn't have a job? To validate his needs, I changed for him; I faked the desire and the lust and privately poured my heart out in journals, desperate to hold on to some part of who I was. Eventually, he got a new job with a massive salary.

"We can finally have the life we deserve," he said when he saw the zeros attached to his pay agreement. "We can set a date now, for the wedding."

I smiled on the outside. My body was massive; long work hours and financial struggles had taken their toll on me. Marrying him was not something that excited me. But I had agreed, and I wore his ring, so we set a date.

Months passed, and I had to maintain my increased workload to pay off the debts—despite his increased income he was not forth-coming with repaying anything. I was tired, unhappy and lost in a permanent fog of worry. He changed toward me as his confidence in work grew. He became his outgoing self again and started socializing with his new work colleagues. Photos would pop up on social media with his arms around glamorous women.

"I'm so glad you're cool about me going out with my workmates; my ex would have gone nuts if she'd seen pictures of me with other women. It's nice to know you trust me."

Then things changed. He stopped talking to me; days would pass with just a grunt. He would complain that there were chocolate bars in the cupboard.

"Who needs to eat this kind of junk? Seriously." The loving stares were replaced with sneers. I felt like the fourteen-year-old girl being summed up for judgment again. I would suggest a night out for a nice meal so that we could reconnect, but he would scream at me: "It's always about food with you."

He was never home; he'd never message. He'd ignore, ignore, ignore. Then came the ridicule, the nastiness, the vile truth of what he was and what I had allowed myself to become.

"You look fucking massive," he said to me one morning, as I stood naked while getting dressed after a particularly emotionless love-making session. He, smug, with "I dare you" eyes, lay on the bed, his hands behind his head.

"What?" I pulled a T-shirt over my belly to cover my shame.

"I said you look fucking massive."

I stood, static in a state of disbelief and confusion. Something inside—anger, rage, utter shock—rose up, and he could tell.

"Oh my God!" His face had the look of a hurt child, flipping with ease from smug to childlike. "You think I called you fat! How? How could you? How could you believe that I would say something like that to you?"

"Er, well, that is what you said." I stood, still naked and now ashamed, though not quite sure of what.

"I meant your tits! Your tits look massive, sexy and full, but no, you think I called you fat. I would never call you fat. Oh my God, I can't believe you think I called you fat."

The word hung like a toxic fume, the bitter repetition of the abuse train: fat, fat, fat, fat ... you ... fat, fat, fat, fat.

My brain heard the words, a subliminal ploy to further crush my self-esteem, to make me lose the value of me and let the flesh I carry over my bones define me. Flesh, in part, put there by him. A few days of being treated like a leper followed, and many, many repetitions of the argument of how he struggled to believe that I loved him when I thought so little of him.

"Fat, fat, you're fat." As often as he could repeat it, his new mantra.

I finally saw him. I saw the abuse. I realized the venomous serpent had crawled up my ample legs and entwined itself around my soul; he was determined to make me fatter and then ensure I hated myself for it.

Years of damaged self-esteem caused by hurtful words from people who I thought loved me had left me open to the ultimate—a damaging, self-serving, manipulative sociopath. I was a meal ticket for him until I wasn't. I lived for nearly eight years with a confused heart and torn feet from dancing on the eggshells that I hadn't even realized were there. He wanted everything I had, and he took it.

It ended in a blur. The swarm of confusion and a drunken argument seemed to bring the woman I was meant to be before the record store to the surface, and I woke one morning finally free: the toxic train had left the station.

Early on after the breakup, I was asked on a couple of dates and went on them. I sat staring at them from across tables and wondered if they would ever get to know me. Would they see beneath the excess flesh? Would they say they love me exactly as I am and then suggest we join a gym or start preparing salads? Would they turn out the light so they didn't have to see my stretch marks? Would they close their eyes when we made love and pretend I was thinner, prettier, someone else? Would they care that I was kind, funny, interesting, passionate and loyal? Would they get to know me before they tried to change me?

The first date ended in a night of *Fifty Shades*–worthy passion, blew the cobwebs away and freed me from the physical memory of the toxic train driver. But after a drunken night and many promises, the next morning he barely touched me. I saw from the corner of my eye that he turned from my wobbly nakedness. He called again a few weeks later, but I made an excuse to decline his invitation for "a bit of fun."

The second date ended with a hug and a swift goodbye. I received a polite message saying he'd like to see me again. I replied saying this was the wrong time and I didn't feel a connection. Abusive messages followed, and I blocked him.

As I politely turned down another date, I realized something. I wasn't just going along with things; I was making choices about what I wanted and whom I would let into my life. It started the path to self-knowledge; it paved the way for freedom from romantic involvement and allowed me to build who I was always meant to be. I had become so defined by fat that I had become like an amoeba with no fixed edges.

In the absence of daily negativity or the distraction of trying to be someone else's everything, I found the little girl who never believed in Prince Charming. Somewhere along the way, she had felt obliged to look for him anyway. I found the slightly chubby girl who had become chubbier with every broken relationship, with every hurtful comment, and I learned to love her.

The parts of me so easily ripped to pieces, like a mismatched jigsaw, suddenly returned with more defined edges. I had been in and out of relationships for over twenty years and had felt compelled by society and family and friends to find someone to complete me, to find someone to love me. I realized the path I needed to take was to feel complete in myself and to figure out who I was.

I learned to accept my body, regardless of its size. I worked with it and started to walk with a friend who listened and laughed with me, someone with no other agenda but to spend time with me and enjoy the outdoors. We went on mountain hikes and stood looking down on the world. We slowly built up our stamina and started running. After a year I completed a half-marathon, just because it was something I'd always wanted to do.

Despite pounds and pounds of excess flesh, I was stronger and fitter than I'd ever been. I learned that our bodies could do great things even if they are big.

I experienced an innate sense of freedom knowing that I could go home to a place that was of my own making, a place where eggshells no longer lay in wait for oblivious toes. I adopted a dog from a rescue centre and learned about companionship and love. I explored who I was and who I wanted to be. I joined a band, started a new business and made a lot of new friends.

When the abuse train left my life, it was loaded with all the comments from my past, every unkind word, hidden insult and well-meaning suggestion. I let it go and blew up the tracks so it can never return. My body is still Big with a capital B, but I have learned to love it. I see past my flesh and allow the woman inside to stand tall. Through self-compassion, I have found joy; through self-acceptance, I found completeness. I don't know how long it'll be before I let someone into my life again, but one thing I do know: he will have to love and respect me the way I have learned to love myself—fucking massively.

FIFTY SHADES OF ~~BLACK~~ FAT: AN INVENTORY

Sonja Boon

"You didn't even try them on. You're just grateful there are T-shirts in your size."

TODAY IT'S JUST YOU AND MARIE KONDO. HANGING OUT TOGETHER. In your closet. Counting.

Black T-Shirts: 10

SOME AREN'T BLACK AT ALL, BUT MORE OF A DULL, DIRTY DARK grey. White spots under the armpits from deodorant. Five years' worth. Of deodorant, that is. You keep them because they have v-necks, and v-necks are "flattering for full-size figures." A headline above some smiling model with red lipstick and shiny hair. Brown, of course, because blond is reserved for thin models. The models don't smile about your other T-shirts. You don't, either. Round neckline. Tight. They strangle but you wear them because you bought them. Five of them, actually. On sale. Size 2X. You didn't even try them on. You're just grateful there are T-shirts in your size. They're not faded. No stains. You'll get used to them. Sometime. Maybe.

YOU'RE TWO IN THE PICTURE. MAYBE YOUNGER. YOUR LEGS ROUND. *Arms rounder. Your face looks like a ripe cherry. Overripe. Bloated. Ready to explode. Your tummy exposed, belly button still a wrinkled outie.*

Later, when you go to school, you stand on the playground, waiting to be invited in. Suck in your tummy. Stand straight. Smile. Be polite. You do everything you're supposed to do, but you're still on the outside. You look at all the other girls standing in a circle, long gangly legs, hair floating in the breeze, clapping to the rhythm of a popular rhyme. You practise at home, just in case you get asked. Tomorrow. Or the day after tomorrow. Or next week. But nobody ever asks. Maybe you haven't sucked your tummy in far enough.

Black Dresses: 4

BLACK. THE SAME DRESS, ACTUALLY. FOUR TIMES. BOUGHT AT Penningtons four years ago. Tents, like giant T-shirts. Two sizes: fat and fat plus, for when you're feeling bloated. Like after Christmas. Or when you're premenstrual. Some pilling where your backpack pulls, but still black after all of these years. You'd wear them every day if you could.

SHE'S LYING ON THE FLOOR WHEN YOU COME IN, A CLUSTER OF GIRLS *around her. Her face is contorted, blood-red lips shaped into a grimace. It takes you a while to figure out what's going on, but when you do, you finally understand. So that's how they do it. That's your first thought. How unbelievably uncomfortable. That's your second. Nope, not doing it. That's your third.*

It's your first week of junior high. Feathered hair. Swear words. Body odour. You haven't bought a curling iron yet. (Braun. Cordless. Butane.)

Makeup is still a few months away, and even then, just a hint of eyeshadow. (Revlon. Moss Green.)

She's wearing white satin pants, those super-tight ones that look like they're painted on. You've seen them in the store. Marvelled at them. But you had no idea how they worked. Now you know. Fashion tips for the uninitiated: White pants for spring and summer. September still counts. When dressing, make yourself horizontal, hook a metal coat hanger into your zipper for leverage, and pull.

Black Leggings: 6 Pairs

WELL, FOUR IF YOU COUNT THE FACT THAT TWO PAIRS HAVE HOLES near the crotch. But then there's the fleece-lined pair that makes winter possible. So, five? Two others are short, for summer. No crotch holes. Seven, then. Black. Do you even need to specify this? Life without leggings would be no life indeed.

YOUR MOM TELLS YOU THAT FAT GIRLS GET THEIR PERIODS EARLY. SHE points to the maxi-pads in the cupboard above the toilet. The one that's up high so nobody will accidentally find them. There's shredded newspaper there, too, she says, so you can wrap them up. You look up at the cupboard and think you'll want the scented pads all the other girls have. Baby powder. Mountain fresh. Spring flowers. The scents waft behind them, marking their arrival into womanhood. One girl gets her period on the exact same day as the sex film in grade five. But your fat body doesn't comply with the rules. You'll be well into thirteen before the baby powder starts wafting around you. By that time the other girls have moved on. That girl in grade five? She's not fat at all.

Black Cardigans: 4

TWO ARE VINTAGE, THE ELBOWS WORN SMOOTH, SHINY. YOU thought they were just old. But last week somebody told you that vintage can apply to things from the eighties, and what do you know, you're slowly becoming trendy again. Bonus. One is lumpy and faded, a little stretched out and a little grey. It's cozier than the dresses. Almost. You bought the new ones online because you hate stores. Just clicked on something and typed in your credit card number. Easy. They were meant for special occasions, but you look like a disgruntled potato in them. Black and rotten. The quality sucks. But still, your size, right?

AT SCHOOL A GIRL YOU'LL CALL AMANDA COMES RUSHING INTO *French class, late. Maybe she ran into a friend. Maybe the bathrooms were full. Maybe her lock got stuck. But everyone else is there already, and the only desk left is the broken one. You know it's broken because one of the sports jocks jumped away before it collapsed on him. And now here's Amanda. Fat. Out of breath. Like you, only more. And everyone knows what's going to happen.*

You can't look away and neither can the rest of the class and you sink into yourself and you can't say anything because there's a code and if you break it you'll become Amanda even though you are already Amanda and so you will yourself into Amanda's mind and hope hope hope she gets the message but she sits down anyway and the desk collapses like everyone knew it would and there's Amanda stuck in the middle, her fat body squeezing out the edges and if this were a car she'd need to get pulled out, Jaws of Life or something, but instead she holds her shame inside and you know because you feel it for her, this body that is too much body that collapses a desk that was already collapsed and the jock laughs because of course he can laugh and then slowly other kids laugh too and you don't but you should have said something but if you had you'd have been laughed at too and so you stay quiet shamed ashamed and you think you might want to talk to Amanda but you know that if it were you you'd rather pretend it didn't happen at all and so you just mumble Hi on the way out. No body is big enough to hold your shame.

Black Jeans: 2 Pairs

ONE PAIR IS FADED ALMOST WHITE WHERE YOUR THIGHS HAVE chafed together on the walk to work. They've been folded in your closet for two years because you hate wearing jeans. They fit, but they pull. They nip. They remind you of your flesh and how it spills up and over. How your organs feel squished inside. They hold you in. Corral you. Contain you. But you don't want to be contained.

YOUR MOM TAPES THE COOKIE TIN SHUT SO YOU CAN'T EAT THEM. AND when she comes home, she counts them, just to make sure. Your parents put a lock on the freezer. They hide the key. The Cinderella cake, a Barbie with a brown chocolate icing skirt flowing around her that's left over from the birthday party, sits in the cold storage. You've secretly been eating cake out the back of her skirt. Your parents casually tell you that she's rotting, making sure that you know that they know you've been snacking on her. Cannibalizing her skirt, her body, her blond hair, her identity. Barbie is slim, her arms graceful, long and white, her pink lips painted into an accommodating smile. You want to be Barbie, but you never had the right one. No Mattel for you. Yours is the cheap plastic one from the store downtown. The one who sits with her hollow legs stretched out wide, vapid vacant orange smile, her dark hair always matted, tangled. Her knees won't bend and she doesn't have a diamond sparkling on her left hand. Her shoes never fit right. She's a cheap knock-off. Maybe that's why Barbie went bad.

Black Socks: A Mystery

HOW DO YOU COUNT SOCKS? YOU DON'T HAVE MATCHING PAIRS.
Mostly you wear mismatched socks. But they're black, so it doesn't
matter. So. Socks: Forty? Twenty pairs? Really? That seems absurd.
You go back and count. At least half have holes where your big toe
has poked through. The twenty socks that remain look like they
come from about fourteen different pairs. You decide not to look too
closely. Ten pairs, then. But maybe it's better just to say twenty. Or
fourteen? You'll figure it out later.

*THE SCALE SAYS YOU'VE GAINED A KILOGRAM. YOUR PARENTS WRITE
this on the calendar in the kitchen and don't say a word.*

Black Underwear: None

YOU DON'T OWN A SINGLE PAIR OF BLACK UNDERWEAR. OR EVEN A
black bra. You bought one, once. La Vie en Rose. Eaton Centre. Toronto.
It was black lace with a clasp in the front. Itchy. Uncomfortable.
Doesn't matter, a friend said. You're not supposed to wear a black lace
bra for a whole night. It's meant to be removed. Sexy. That bra isn't
for you; it's for your lover. You'd never even considered that possibility. Your underwear is functional. Comfortable. Cotton. Pale pink
flowers. Light blue stripes. Lavender. Colour coordinated in packs
of five. Why does underwear need to coordinate with itself? Also,
almost forgot: two black slips. Torn. You haven't had the energy to
pick up new ones so you just mush them into the elastic waistband
of your skirt. It's black, too. Naturally.

WHAT'S THE EQUATION FOR LOVE? IF YOU LOSE WEIGHT, YOU'LL BE more attractive. Maybe you'll have a boyfriend, even. You learned that lesson a long time ago. But do you want one? It occurs to you that the boyfriends in your imagination are better than the boyfriends your friends talk about in real life. You retreat into your books.

Over the years, you learned to hide. Erase your self. You figured out that if you wore black, you could do a good job of fading into the background. Layers. Camouflage. Until now, it's worked.

Your husband tells you you're his most valuable asset, his hands running along the curves of your left leg. Almost twenty-five years of marriage and you shy away. Unsure. He likes having something to hold on to. Your skin is so soft, he says. Like bread dough just before you set it to rise. Warm. Yeasty. Malleable. Fleshy. Ripe. He looks at you with wonder and you look away.

$$10 + 4 + 7 + 4 + 20 + 2 + 2 + 1 = 50. \text{ SPARKING JOY?}$$

WHEN YOU LOOK BACK AT OLD SCHOOL PICTURES, YOU SEE THAT there wasn't much stomach to suck in at all. In your memories, you reach for the odd one out, standing on the edges, her shoulders hunched by her ears, holding her breath. Silent, because if she talked, she wouldn't have been able to suck in that tummy. Or stand straight. Not really. You wonder what might have happened if she'd opened her mouth, breathed, spoken.

SUPER PLUS SIZE ME

Jessie Blair

"My next weigh-in was a few months after surgery. ...
I held my breath as I stepped onto the scale."

I SCREAMED AS THE PAIN SHOT THROUGH MY LOWER BACK. FAST as a lightning bolt, it knocked me to the living room floor. I lay on the beige carpet for an hour curled up like a dried autumn leaf. Each time I tried to uncurl myself, as slowly as I could, the pain stopped me from moving again. My eyes turned red from crying, and I could feel the congestion inside my nasal passages building up until my ears felt completely plugged.

At last I stood up and steadied myself with my hand against a wall. The muscles in my lower back and right leg spasmed. I looked down the hallway to the bathroom. The pain made the hallway look as though I were peering through shards of broken glass—everything seemed farther away, a little crooked and in pieces. I held my hands to the wall and walked very slowly, step by step toward the bathroom. When I got to the door, I held on to the frame with one hand and slowly reached over with the other hand to place it on the sink counter. My right hand shook as I lifted it to open the medicine cabinet and dispense some Tylenol. Then I slowly made my way to the bed and collapsed.

My husband, David, took me to the doctor the next day. My legs shook as David walked arm in arm with me to guide me to the car.

He very gently got me seated and then pulled out the seat belt and buckled me in. Once at the office, my doctor was concerned enough to order an MRI, and I was diagnosed with osteoarthritis in several spots along the lumbar of my spine. I was prescribed painkillers and referred to physiotherapy and a back specialist. The doctor told me it would be good for me to lose weight.

When I was younger, I could move more, so it was easier to lose weight if I stayed active and was careful of what I ate. But now, at 320-plus pounds and with a serious mobility issue, moving long enough to lose weight without experiencing strain on my back was harder. I began using walking poles for balance whenever I needed to walk more than a few blocks. I knew I had to do something, and weight-loss surgery was an obvious route to go. Had I not been in so much pain, I might not have gone the route of surgery, but the quality of my life was at stake.

After two years on the waiting list, I was looking forward to meeting the surgeon who would be doing a gastric sleeve on my stomach. The day before the appointment, David put the last of the luggage into the car trunk while I slipped into the car. My hands were shaking as he closed the door and started the engine. A thousand what-ifs flooded my mind.

I looked at David and said, "What if the surgery doesn't work?"

"I have watched you struggle with your weight and face disappointments. This is an opportunity for change, and we will make it successful together."

During the previous two years I was prescribed Victoza to help curb my appetite and lose weight. I was hoping that would be enough and that I wouldn't need the surgery in the end. I'd managed to lose twenty pounds and maintain the weight loss, but that wasn't enough to yield much relief to my stressed spine. I felt disappointed that I hadn't lost more. Though I was discouraged, surgery was worth a try.

I drew in deeper breaths as we approached the ferry at Tsawwassen heading to Swartz Bay on Vancouver Island. I lived in Vancouver, and the hospital was ninety-five kilometres away. The ferry ride across the water is an hour and a half long—plenty of time to fret about all that could go wrong. The final wait seemed interminable, especially since I couldn't be sure the surgeon would accept me as his patient.

When I reached the surgeon's office, I was quickly ushered into a stark white examination room. The surgeon popped in ten minutes later. We chatted for about half an hour and then he said, "I think you're ready for surgery. I will get my secretary to schedule a time. Make sure you lose at least twenty more pounds before surgery."

He said that would reduce the risk of accidentally cutting nearby organs. I breathed a sigh of relief. I'd been approved—with a contingency, of course.

When I got home, I was motivated to lose the weight. For the next week I was diligent about going to the gym and watching what I ate. By the sixth day I was feeling tired, though, and my back was sore. I decided to skip a day at the gym and rest. Then day two of rest went by, then day three, and I became frustrated with myself and angry about my feelings of laziness.

I got the call from the secretary a few days later. She told me the date of the surgery. I noted it was just a month away and told myself I'd better get on the ball. But I just couldn't. I hurt too much.

I followed up with my doctor's office a week later. To ensure I was ready for the surgery, the nurse went over the instructions for preparation. "Mrs. Blair, please start your liquid diet two weeks prior to surgery. Please don't have any caffeine during this time." My eyes got wide and I panicked at the thought of no coffee. "Only decaf."

"Well, at least I get to try to fool my body," I said with a giggle.

When it came time to weigh in, I drew in several deep breaths. Part of me wanted to know if I had been successful losing weight, and the other part of me didn't want to know. The numbers on the scale said that I was down by only five pounds.

I exhaled an "Oh."

The nurse looked at me, finished logging my weight-loss numbers and said, "You sound disappointed."

"The surgeon wanted me to lose twenty pounds."

Much to my relief, she said, "I wouldn't worry about it. During the liquid-diet phase you will lose a lot of weight."

I relaxed a little and set my mind to focusing on staying on a liquid diet for two weeks. David insisted on preparing my foods. In twenty-three years of marriage to him, I have never tired of his doting.

The diet consisted of Premier Protein shakes, up to three a day; half a cup of broth; one cup of decaf coffee with cream; water; and specially formulated meal replacement packages that could be turned into shakes. David meticulously measured all my foods and put my daily allotment on one side of the kitchen counter for me. Since the first day wasn't too bad, I thought that this might be easier to do than I'd expected.

By the end of day five, however, I felt tired of the liquids and wanted real food. David reminded me that I didn't have that far to go until the surgery, that I was almost halfway through the liquid diet.

"Hang in there," he said. "Otherwise you'll only regret your decision."

He was right. No second chances. If I didn't get through this preparation stage to the surgery, I was pretty sure I would be wait-listed again for another several years. I was determined to make this chance work so I wouldn't have to go through this again.

By the time day twelve rolled around, I had adjusted, though I was still feeling very hungry. My body and mind were craving the chewing motion that comes with having solid foods. Someone suggested that I try chewing gum. That suggestion saw me through to the day of surgery—day fifteen.

On that day I could have only a little bit of water and nothing else. After all, they were going to be cutting my stomach and they wanted it empty. I heard my stomach complaining and felt its rumbles. The smell of disinfectant filled my nostrils as I walked into the operating room in my blue hospital gown, cap and slippers. The nurse and the surgeon, who were already there waiting for me, greeted me when I arrived.

I worried: What if something goes wrong and I have horrible digestive issues after surgery? Followed by a reassuring thought: You're here now; just do it. Everything will be fine.

I got up on the table and the anesthesiologist hooked me up to saline solution and heart monitor equipment to prep me for surgery. That went fine, but when the specialist put the IV into my vein, crimson-red blood suddenly poured onto the floor. She was horrified for making a mistake, but not as horrified as I was. I watched helplessly as my blood splashed onto the floor and splattered in different directions. However, the specialist and staff quickly cleaned up the spill and fixed the IV.

After that, I was surprised how easily I shrugged it off. The specialist instructed me to lie back on the table. Soon after, I saw the specialist's face come into view as she put a mask on my face. I heard her instruct me to count backwards from ten. I don't remember closing my eyes at all.

When I opened my eyes again, the ceiling lights looked blurry. My eyesight adjusted as I looked around the room. A nurse came to ask me how I was feeling and if I was ready for water. I could drink only water for the first few hours after surgery. The staff wanted to monitor how well my body would tolerate water before giving me anything else. The only thought I had at that moment was that I wanted food, solid food—like a big, juicy, thick hamburger. Instead, when food came about two hours later, I was given broth and Jell-O, with instructions to eat only two tablespoons of broth every hour.

My hand shook with hunger as I brought the first tablespoon of broth to my lips. The smell of the chicken broth made me salivate. Once I'd taken the second tablespoon, I placed my spoon on the tray and David pushed it away from me so I wouldn't be tempted to eat more. This pattern repeated several times for the next twelve hours.

The next morning, my stomach grumbled. I was irritable and so very hungry. The hospital staff encouraged me to walk up and down the halls during my surgical recovery, and I did so several times. I stopped to chat with one of my weight-loss surgery buddies I knew from the orientation class at the hospital. She was not doing well. She couldn't keep the broth down. Suddenly, a wave of gratitude vibrated through my entire being. I was well on my way to recovery, but she was still struggling to keep food down.

Breakfast was no different from the night before—broth, Jell-O and tea—but I could eat the entire meal, albeit very slowly. A few sips here, a teaspoon of Jell-O there, and an hour later I was finished breakfast. Just as I pushed the tray aside, the surgeon entered the room to see how my recovery was going. He was pleased with my progress.

As he was leaving the room, he turned around to look at me.

"The surgery went well," he said as he adjusted his glasses, "although you were still a little too large going into the operation. You know, if this surgery doesn't work there's nothing else I can do for you. This is your only chance."

My eyebrows furrowed as I looked back at him, thinking, I'm aware that if this doesn't work, I'm out of options. Why do you think I did it? If there had been other options, I would have taken them.

The surgeon's words seemed unnecessarily cruel. I felt like a kid who just had an encounter with the schoolyard bully. But I recovered myself and decided to get fully behind my decision. You've got this, I told myself.

I spent the next week recovering at my brother's home in Victoria. David and I got outside for short walks every day, and wherever we walked there seemed to be deer. I took a lot of photos with my phone's camera and oohed and aahed at the cute critters. My recovery environment was calm and nurturing, just as every patient should experience.

The liquid diet expanded as more items, such as rice cereal and protein powder, were added. I had to ensure I was getting lots of protein since my doctor's main concern was that my body would start losing muscle if I didn't get enough. David was diligent about measuring out the right amount of protein and ensuring that I had enough to eat and drink. He had taken time off work to help me through my recovery period. I was truly grateful for him.

The procedure I had was called laparoscopic surgery. The surgeon made small incisions around the stomach area, pumped my abdomen with a type of gas so he could see where to cut the stomach and then stitched me back up. The incisions were made right under my breasts, so for the first week I couldn't wear a bra because everything was too tender. Whenever I went outside, I bundled up well and then put a cape overtop to try to conceal the fact that I was braless. Even with all that concealment, I still felt embarrassed about being braless. I was anxious that people would judge me for it. I expressed my concerns to David.

"The last thing I need right now is additional judgment," I told him. "I do enough of that for myself."

"Most people aren't seeking to harm others. I don't think they'll judge you, but if they do, they'll regret it because they'll have to deal with me," he said as he helped me put on my coat.

I hoped not. I didn't need added stress coming from the outside. This whole process was stressful enough. I knew I would be stronger later, but for now I needed to feel safe and secure while healing.

After a week of recovering in Victoria, we travelled back home to Vancouver. By that time, I was tired of eating whey protein powder in my broth, yogurt and protein drinks. I was ready for something more substantial. I began having small portions of puréed meat and vegetables in addition to what was already on my menu. I added whey protein powder to the puréed foods as well. Unfortunately, the powder gave everything a lumpy, white, pasty look, and it overpowered the bland foods. Everything tasted like what I imagined chalk would taste like.

On the day after I was allowed solid food, I ate too quickly because I was so hungry. Desperately hungry. Suddenly, my food, trying to fit through a narrow door to my stomach, got caught. It felt as though the door to my stomach had slammed shut and then began cramping as the food tried to get unstuck from the stomach's doorway. When the food fell into my stomach all at once, I quickly ran to the washroom, where my stomach discharged all the food. I was in pain and chagrined that I'd been in a hurry when I knew better.

Lesson learned: don't eat so fast. After that experience, I stayed on a puréed diet for at least a week before going back to solid foods.

My next weigh-in was a few months after surgery to find out how I was progressing and if there were any problems. I held my breath as I stepped onto the scale. My eyes followed the needle as it bounced from number to number until it rested on 260 pounds.

Closing my eyes, I felt my chest deflate with a heavy sigh. When I reopened my eyes, they were filled with tears. My nose felt congested. Frustration set in. What in the hell was the point of measuring food, and all those hours sweating at the gym, if the result wasn't significant weight loss?

Later that day, I left my house to go meet a friend for coffee. The café had an outdoor patio covered by a green awning and had white tables and chairs. The decor made me feel as though I had been transported to Paris. The smell of cinnamon buns welcomed me as I entered the café. I looked around the establishment until I came eye to eye with my friend, and we greeted each other with smiles.

We exchanged a hug when I got to the table. My friend is a tall, beautiful, plump woman with black, shoulder-length, curly hair, the biggest brown eyes and dark skin. When the waitress came by, we both ordered lemon cake and coffee.

"I may as well have what I want since I can't seem to lose weight," I said as I rolled my eyes. "I measure everything I eat, and I work out almost every day."

My friend nodded her head in agreement.

"I've been thinking about weight lately," she replied. "I think it may be more beneficial for us to acknowledge that eating and exercising are acts of self-care instead of means to an end. Perhaps we need to be thankful for those acts of self-care instead of feeling disappointed when weight loss doesn't occur."

I'd never thought of eating and exercise that way. My eyebrows rose toward the sky, and I smiled while I let her words seep in. My jaw unclenched and I let deep breaths of relief plunge into my lungs. I could see myself smiling in my mind's eye at the notion of self-care taking precedence over disappointment. We ate our cake—I ate mine slowly—and talked for hours. When we left the café, I was smiling. I'd made a shift.

A few months later, I weighed in and discovered I had hit 250 pounds, the smallest I had been in a long time. The nurse said I weighed 299 pounds going into surgery, so I had lost 49 pounds since the procedure six months prior.

"That's good progress. Congratulations, Jessie!"

I smiled and acknowledged that I had done well.

Slow and steady progress is better than no progress at all. My back is getting better, and I am feeling stronger every day. I continue to lose weight slowly toward my goal of 170 pounds. Once I reach that weight-loss goal, I will do all I can to maintain it. I will never have a lean, athletic body because I am not built that way. I can be happy being my slightly chubby and active self again—focusing on self-care instead of numbers.

SIZE ME UP

Heather van Mil

"From the tips of my size 11 feet to the top of my five-foot-eleven head, everything about me screams big."

MY FIRST MEMORY OF BODY AWARENESS COMES FROM WHEN I WAS ten. I had an eighteen-year-old sister I idolized. She was everything I wanted to be when I grew up, so every night for over a year I prayed two very specific prayers with fervour:

1. I prayed that I would have big boobs.
2. I prayed that I would not be fat.

More to the point, I prayed that I would have a very flat stomach. I didn't care how wide I was, I just really wanted a flat stomach in profile. That was how specific the image was that I had in my head.

Spoiler alert: I got the big boobs. I didn't get the flat stomach. At least I never "felt" like I had a flat stomach. That may sound like a weak statement, but I have come to realize that it makes all the difference. Let me tell you why.

I have always been very size conscious. Everyone says that the number on the clothes means nothing, because it is so subjective. One brand's size 12 is another brand's size 8. Cognitively I know that, but getting my heart on board is a whole different ball game. There are four sizes that have been permanently imprinted in my brain, on my heart and soul:

– 4 –

THAT WAS THE SIZE OF THE BRIDESMAID DRESS I WORE AT MY SIS-ter's wedding. I was fourteen, in grade nine and just starting to be conscious of, and care about, the size of my clothes. I still have that dress. Not because it's beautiful; it is not. It's aubergine and has shoulder pads. I kept it to prove to myself, someone else, the world, I don't know—that at one point I was a size 4. In my way of thinking, it didn't matter that I was practically prepubescent, with a lot of grow-ing left to do. It was a badge to wear. I wasn't always fat. I used to be a size 4. I'm one of you in hiding!

– 16 –

THAT'S BEEN THE SIZE OF MY CLOTHES FOR THE MAJORITY OF MY teen and adult life. When I am active but still eating what I enjoy, this is where my body naturally rests. I'm a tall, big girl, and it makes sense. It was a difficult size to wear, because many "straight sizes" didn't go up that high (especially not in the nineties), and many plus sizes didn't go that low.

– 10 –

THAT IS THE SIZE I WAS WHEN I WAS FIVE MONTHS PREGNANT WITH my first child. I was so ill that I vomited upwards of twenty times per day. I had lost over thirty pounds in six weeks. My hip bones stuck out like mountains over the valley where my baby bump should have been, and I had caverns in my collarbones. My cheekbones were defined in my previously round face, and I had a jawbone that could cut glass. My sister came for a visit and told me that I looked like a model.

I was thrilled.

– 24 –

THIS IS THE SIZE I AM NOW. ONE SIZE FOR EACH OF THE TWENTY years since I wore that awful size 4 bridesmaid dress. I should be wiser now with the accumulation of years, and weight. So what have I learned?

I've learned that I feel fat no matter what size I am. From my skinniest to my fattest, from my fittest to my laziest, from my healthiest to my sickest. I always thought I was too big. The only time, and I mean truly the only time, I have *ever* felt "normal" (i.e., as thin as everyone else, as thin as I "should be") was when I was so sick that I was almost hospitalized. I vomited everything that went near my lips, but I looked great! Or so I thought. The scary thing was that the world thought so, too. I got so much affirmation everywhere I went and from everyone I came into contact with.

I've always joked that being pregnant was the best diet I ever did, certainly the only diet that was ever successful. The vicious sickness—hyperemesis gravidarum, now made famous by Kate Middleton—was my golden ticket to thinness. That joke hid the frustration of a body that works seemingly in reverse of how it is supposed to. That joke hid the shame of seeing people who once exclaimed how great I looked for just having given birth now puzzle at how I could possibly have fallen so far, so fast.

But where does that leave me now? I still have a complicated relationship with my weight and my size. I still wish I were as "fat" as

I used to think I was when I was a size 16. I looked good. But if I ever got back there, would I appreciate it? How do I fix this broken brain of mine? How do I navigate my heavy load through a society that praises me when I'm sick and shames me when I'm healthy(ish)?

Barring surgery, it's unlikely that I'll ever be a size 16 again. In addition to the two pregnancies that destroyed my metabolism and my muscle mass (not to mention my tooth enamel and my cavity-free record), I have had two knee dislocations that left me immobile for long stretches of time and led to the discovery of a hypermobility disorder that renders me unable to do most forms of exercise for fear of more dislocations. Add on top of that two car accidents that have gifted me with chronic pain, and it equals out to a lot of weight piled on, and not many options to shift it.

I have become disciplined enough with the exercise I can do that were I currently a size 16, I might be able to maintain it—but getting enough momentum to lose the weight is so unlikely. I have never been very disciplined with my eating, and, facing a lifetime of chronic pain plus the depression and anxiety that come with that, it's highly doubtful that I'll solve my broken relationship with food in this lifetime.

SO WHAT DOES ALL OF THIS MEAN? AM I DESTINED TO BE A SIZE 24 for the rest of my life? Or more? How likely is it that I'll never gain another pound, or another inch? How do I raise two daughters with healthy self-esteem and body positivity when I've never had either? Some days these questions are enough to leave me frozen with fear, or despairing beyond measure. Some days I see a glimmer of light at the end of the tunnel when my ten-year-old loves her amazing six-pack and my soft belly with equal passion.

I've only recently come to realize that my weight and dress size are only part of the equation. One of the—pun intended—BIG reasons that I felt out of sync with the rest of society is all of the other ways I am too big. From the tips of my size 11 feet to the top of my five-foot-eleven head, everything about me screams big, even when I was a size 4. My height is too big. My feet are too big. My voice is too big. My hands are too big. My laugh is too big. My mouth is definitely too big. My cheeks are too big. My nose is too big. Even my eyebrows used to be too big. None of that was changed by being fatter or thinner.

How did I go from being the ten-year-old who idolized her big sister (who is also "too big" in many of the same ways I am) to being the adult who feels so uncomfortable in the body she prayed fervently for?

It's easy to blame my petite mother, who, at five feet, two inches and goodness knows what tiny dress size, refused to wear a bathing suit when we went camping because she hated her body so much. It's easy to blame my family, which placed food at the centre of every occasion, every emotion, be it happy, sad, boring, angry or anything in between. It's easy to blame the childhood trauma that comes with being raised by an alcoholic father. It's easy to blame my financial situation. If I had the money to have a personal trainer to whip me into shape with all of my physical limitations, had a chef to cook healthy meals, and could afford all the best, high-quality, nutritious food, then maybe I'd be skinny. Or hello, plastic surgery!

It's easy to blame a society that screams "You are unlovable, disgusting, lazy and worse" at me from every poster, magazine, commercial, TV show and movie I encounter. It's easy to blame a fashion industry that encourages straight-sized women to be sexy and flaunt their assets, and plus-sized women to wear muumuus and cover themselves up.

It's easy to blame myself. It's really easy to blame myself.

Why does there need to be blame? Why are some illnesses moralized in this way? Do we blame someone when they are blind or deaf? No one says, "Wow, they must be really lazy," or "If you only did x, y and z, then you would be able to see again." It's absurd, but that is what we do with overweight and obese people. It is a personal and moral failing, instead of a symptom of an illness that needs treating.

Sometimes I feel the need to wear a T-shirt that outlines all of my illnesses so I won't be judged as one of *those fat people*. That makes me just as bad as any skinny judgmental person. No matter how someone arrives at an overweight or obese place, judgment and shame are not going to cure them. So what will?

If you have read this looking for answers, I'm afraid I'm going to disappoint you. If I had the answers, I might be skinny. Or maybe I'd still be fat, but finally at peace with myself. I am neither of those things.

What I am is exhausted. Carrying the physical and emotional load that I do is incredibly soul crushing. Sometimes I put on a happy face and wear a bikini to the beach, despite my mother's lack of example. Sometimes I wear size 4X sweatpants and lie in bed for days at a time. Sometimes I get in front of the camera in my lingerie and feel beautiful. Sometimes I cringe when I see photos of me fully clothed and delete them. Sometimes I get the short haircut that I love in the summer, no matter my face shape. Sometimes I wear my hair long and straight in an effort to hide my multiple chins.

Sometimes I dream of having plastic surgery. They have a name for it, you know. The "mommy makeover": a tummy tuck and a breast lift, with a side of liposuction. If you're lucky, you can get it at the same time as your c-section. Sometimes I'm ashamed for dreaming of plastic surgery. After all, I'm raising two girls. I don't want them to think everyone should look the same, do I? I don't want them to think the solution for body-image issues is plastic surgery, do I? They love my squishy tummy; why can't I? But what if they don't? They're only young still. Soon enough they will be teenagers and will probably be embarrassed by my squishy tummy instead of loving it.

I guess my point in telling you all of this is to say that the only person's perception I can control is my own. When I was younger, I didn't have control of my perception. I wasn't even aware of it. And in this same way, to an extent, I can shape my children's perceptions for the time being, and I hope with every fibre of my being that I am using that power for good instead of evil.

IT SOUNDS CLICHÉ, BUT IT REALLY IS ALL IN YOUR HEAD. NO MATter what clothing size I've been, I've felt fat. I've felt too big. And yes, there are people in the world who will share that same perception. They will look at me and decide that I am fat, and they don't like it. They may even feel the need to tell me that. But people can just as easily judge me for other things that are out of my control. They might not like my gender, or my age, or my eye colour. They might not like things that *are* in my control, like my career, the way I raise my children or my taste in music, and I certainly don't lose sleep over that.

Don't get me wrong. Some perceptions are more harmful than others. Yes, we can strive to let hurtful comments roll off our backs with much of the population, but at the same time, we do still need to advocate unbiased health care and an otherwise more inclusive society at large.

But, for now, I will continue to ignore every fibre of my being that is shouting hateful things at me. I will take a deep breath and ignore your side-eye and arched eyebrows. I'll be damned if I let them stop me from enjoying my ice cream in my bikini at the beach with my kids. Size me up all you want; I don't even know what size that bikini is. Yes, my stretch marks and rolls are on display for everyone to see. And damn, that sun feels good.

5FB

Cassie Stocks

"It's the fear that I will look a fool. ... I will look like a brocade sofa, a walking, overstuffed backpack with zippers and buckles."

MY WALLET AND WAISTLINE ARE SKEWED TOWARD WALMART, plus-sized section, clearance racks. But I love beautiful clothing, designer clothing: Ann Demeulemeester (think Patti Smith, her black blazers and perfect white shirts), Dries Van Noten (1920s tweeds mixed with patterned brocades and silks), Yohji Yamamoto (angular, cutting-edge designs), Dolce & Gabbana (everything over the top in a fabulously subversive way).

I sit in front of the computer, my cat trying to crawl up my back, and flip through runway shots on the *Vogue* site, sighing at the construction, the tailoring and the quality of fabrics. I plunk the cat on the floor and venture to a linked shopping site. That wonderful Demeulemeester blazer costs $1,254. Largest size is an 8; it might fit the cat.

At the end of all the runway galleries, there's always a final photo of the designer coming out to take a bow—a designer often three times the size of the largest range their clothing comes in. What's that about? You design clothing you could never wear? Oh, I detest them. Of course, they just have the workers whip them up custom outfits, leaving all the other larger ladies (even those with possible purchasing means) weeping in their overflowing linen closets (or sumptuous walk-in closets, as the case may be).

I allow myself transitory fantasies of a fashion-designer kidnapping. Transporting him in the back seat of my car, his arms and legs tied with silken ribbons, black satin bag over his head (so as not to chafe). I ignore his neurotic griping in Italian or some other fashionably foreign language. Once he is released to the chair in front of my sewing machine, I'd allow the cat to climb on him, and flap pages of a swanky clothing magazine in his face. "Sew me this, asshole. In my size. And it better look good."

I dismiss the fantasy not only because I can't afford the gas to make it to New York but because I imagine trauma is not conducive to creativity and I may end up with nothing but a puddle of designer widdle on my living room floor.

I come to believe that the only way I will ever have the style of clothes I covet is to sew them myself. I will become my own designer. My personal clothing line will be called 5FB: Fashion for a Financially Fraught, Fat, Fifty-Year-Old Bohemian. I begin to slowly collect fabric and patterns, watch sewing videos and read reviews of patterns. My linen closet becomes filled with frustration and hundreds of dollars of fabric (all the softer to weep upon), patterned silk from Uzbekistan, linen in black, blue and brown, paisley polyester from the thrift store. Stacks of potential fabulousness waiting for nothing but courage. For me to finally decide that my thighs deserve high-quality linen, that I am brave enough to commence this 5FB sewing project.

I do not begin. Why? Because I will judge my efforts against those runway photos. I will want impeccable tailoring, French seams and welt pockets. I will want the clothing to hang on my rotund body exactly as it does on the fashion-model waifs. I will want perfection. And I will not get it. The same reason that brought forth the desire to produce stops the production—the size and shape of my body. Oh, perfection, you damnable noun. I continue my studies, postponing the actual with the theoretical. Then comes the horrifying realization that these envelopes with my sizes on the front (and terrifying hieroglyphic symbols inside) still will not fit properly.

I read that I will need to learn to do pattern adjustments, perhaps for a Protruding Derrière, Round Tummy, Bulging Thighs or Broad Shoulders and, in my case, almost certainly a Full Bust Adjustment. An FBA involves some sort of mathematical (screw math) calculation based on my apparently oversized bustline versus the pattern cup size, and then performing a slash and pivot operation on the pattern. I feel like a freak even in my own sizing. The solution may be to just slash the patterns completely in some sort of sewing killer rage, leaving strafed waftings of tissue paper whirling around the room.

The rage is real, and born of my self-doubt. The idea that I will never be as beautiful, successful or well dressed as the thin. Never. And I fight, wrestle those skinny demons to the ground, and they get back up again, bolstered by advertising everywhere, by dismissive glances that take in my body size before I even open my mouth, by stores filled with millions of items that I cannot wear. I start from behind (a behind needing a Protruding Derrière adjustment, apparently) and fight to be taken seriously, to be noticed, to be heard. And isn't that a part of the sewing concept? The idea that my clothing will broadcast to others that someone, somewhere, believes I am worthy of quality? That someone believes my sizable self deserves to be noticed, to be cutting-edge, silk and brocade fabulous. The ideal, to wear something that puts me out front, not bringing up the rear, where I have already been dismissed.

I work these things through in my head, the courage to begin, to accept that I may make mistakes, the belief that I'm worthy. Right, okay, I'm ready. Or not. An invisible wraith-like worry slips under the door. The cat is oblivious, as usual, to everything but the sound of the can opener. It's the fear that I will look a fool. That I will make a mockery of myself. In drawing attention to myself, I increase the risk of negative attention. I will look like a brocade sofa, a walking, over-stuffed backpack with zippers and buckles, an unmetamorphosed caterpillar pretending to be a butterfly. The risk is, at the front, you may get shot down; perhaps it is better to stay hidden in the trenches at the back of the battlefield. 5FB: Fashion for a Freakish, Foolish, Fat, Fifty-Year-Old Bozo.

Fuck. And then: fuck it. What do they say? No guts, no glory. A true soldier does not admit defeat before the battle. I shall defend my fashion, whatever the cost may be, I shall fight in the bistros, I shall fight in the meeting rooms, I shall fight on the buses and in the supermarkets, I shall fight in the bathrooms; I shall never surrender. Though I might go have a gin. Perfection is for the perfect, and none of us is. Not the svelte, the wealthy or the famous. We are all battling doubts and fighting fears from the front of the room and the back.

I shall begin. A silk flak jacket? Camouflage jumpsuit? Something simple, something that may, in some way, succeed. I read the pattern instructions twice and place the fabric on my table. "Well, cat," I say, "it's time to cut." The cat jumps up, lies on the fabric and then rolls happily, the carefully prewashed, preshrunk material wrinkled and covered in cat hair before I even start. I plonk the cat on the floor. I begin.

THE WEIGHT OF MOTHERHOOD

Jennifer Pownall

"When I lost weight ... I did not become a
more impressive human being."

I PUT MOTHERHOOD ON HOLD IN ORDER TO LOSE WEIGHT. FOR ME, it was a question of health. And a desire to have a healthy pregnancy.

My husband, Evan, and I had been married for a year and were beginning to discuss the likelihood of starting a family. We had been fortunate in having the opportunity to have a proper honeymoon, and we had gone on a cruise for our first anniversary. We were deeply in love and felt the ticking of the clock, as many not-quite-so-young couples do. We were happily mentally preparing to exchange hand holding for diaper changing, to trade mornings snuggled together in bed for sleepless nights comforting a newborn.

We had been chatting and planning for a couple of months when I went to my standing appointment to donate blood. I was halted at the nurse's station by a blood-pressure reading slightly too low to be acceptable for me to proceed with the donation. "Go for a walk around the block" was the friendly advice. "It will raise the number and we should be able to go ahead." I did and it did, and I gave blood as per usual.

But when I got home, I made the mistake of doing an online search for "low blood pressure." A sobbing phone call to my husband half an hour into my investigation and he suddenly found himself in full reassurance mood. "Yeah, babe, I know sometimes your pulse races too ... Well, the nurses didn't seem very concerned ... No, sweetheart, you're not going to die ..." His practised comfort was the balm I needed to soothe the cutting anxieties of my hypochondria.

When he got home that evening, his warm arms around me felt like the final punctuation on our earlier conversation. But he offered one follow-up thought that turned out to be a significant catalyst: "When you're pregnant you can't go online for stuff like this. If you look up every burp or hiccup you'll always be in a panic, and that won't be healthy for you or the baby."

He was right. I was the first to admit that I had a tendency to work myself up, and being worried about every tiny symptom of pregnancy would do nothing but make things worse. I was not ignorant of the connection between obesity and health problems, and it was this link that had long been the unshooable fly of my mind. I knew if I could lose the extra weight, I would eliminate most of my health anxieties. And preparing for the responsibility of carrying a child, whose well-being depended upon my own, was exactly the motivation I needed to kick my weight-loss efforts into high gear.

The next day, I spoke with Evan, explaining how his words had affected me and inspired a level of commitment I was certain I had never known. I asked for the time I needed to lose the weight, and together we decided to hold off on trying for one more year.

I began walking each day. Occasionally, if it was raining or my motivation was particularly lacking, I would lower my considerable curves to the carpet to practise awkward crunches, or satisfy my dedication to move more by repeatedly trudging up and down the stairs to our attic. I cut up days' worth of fresh vegetables at a time to always have a healthy snack at the ready, and I stopped shopping the inner aisles of the grocery store, instead filling my cart from the perimeter with simple, whole foods.

I shed fifty pounds before anyone other than my husband mentioned noticing the change. I think a lot of people sense that "You look like you've lost weight" can be a dangerous comment when directed to someone who has spent years on the lose-gain elevator.

I KEPT AT IT.

Wraps had become a quick favourite, but I became more enterprising with what I stuffed into them, the seams sometimes bursting with slivers of bright red pepper or the flat, tufted, green leaves of cilantro. I began to use a step aerobics DVD as part of my normal workout routine, found my old dumbbells and rediscovered a whole range of muscles I had long forgotten. I started jogging intermittently when I walked, eventually—with my husband working out at my side—tackling a program meant to slowly increase run time until participation in a 5K became a possibility. I did a 5K, and then another where I won first place for my category. Eventually, we both ran a 10K in under an hour, and I began to entertain the idea of a half-marathon. Girlfriends started asking me to go shopping. I became more adventurous, feeling freer in a lighter body, and I tried new activities like dragon boating and ziplining. Evan and I enjoyed a more energetic sex life.

But loved ones also began to offer me food right up to my lips. With images of my former obese self so fresh in their minds, they insisted that I must be close to my target weight and wondered aloud if I was losing too much. The truth was, my body mass index still held me in the "overweight" category. But at only the six-month mark, I celebrated the loss of 100 pounds. The next month I was down another 10, and I duplicated those results in the five weeks that followed. Nine months into my journey, I was 124 pounds lighter than my highest weight, and nestled nicely in the upper half of the "normal" category for my body mass index.

I was aware certain people looked at me differently. I knew I did. Evan had shed 50 pounds himself, so the two of us, anticipating the cry of a newborn in our near future, took a few extra months to enjoy the leaner bodies we had worked so hard to procure. But eventually we knew the time was right. I had worked tirelessly in pursuit of a body I was confident would allow for the healthiest pregnancy, and it was time to allow it to shine in the role for which it had been shaped.

I was a lean, mean baby-making machine.

BUT THE LESSONS OF MY LIFE HAVE ALWAYS CENTRED ON MY expectations. Six weeks after we started trying, I was pregnant. Our lightness and joy lasted just days, though, before the bleeding began. After an ultrasound, followed by a drive to the emergency room, I was admitted to the hospital in preparation for surgery. The pregnancy was ectopic, and allowing the baby to continue growing within my Fallopian tube would have meant not just its death but mine as well. I was told there was no choice.

Grief is a word that cannot possibly contain all the wounds of child loss.

We were devastated, and felt doubly impacted by what had happened because of the surgical ramifications that left me in a great deal of pain and under orders to do nothing. I felt deficient—like I was a woman incapable of doing what women are innately able to do. I felt like my body had betrayed me. And I was too keenly aware of the stinging irony of my failure to sustain a pregnancy within the healthiest form I could possibly offer.

I had set fire to my very home and was only then realizing that to rebuild did not guarantee immunity to new flames.

I HAD TO FOLLOW UP WITH A SERIES OF BLOOD TESTS AND VISITS to a specialized clinic. I was informed that my HCG—the hormone associated with pregnancy—levels were still rising. They had failed to remove all the tissue during surgery, and the remaining cells were continuing to replicate within my tube. I was still at risk. I was injected with a chemotherapy agent and told not to be alone. I was not to walk anywhere or jostle myself in any way, lest I trigger a rupture.

I felt like a prisoner of my environment, my body, my mind and emotions. I was overwhelmed by the lack of control I held over what was happening, and so I turned—as I so often had in past periods of depression or anxiety—to food.

There is an emotional component to eating that is so much more fulfilling than anything we put into our mouths or bodies. For many people who feel swept along by the current of life, it can be the one thing that most closely resembles a preserver when our heads are all but drowned just below those raging waters. The problem is, as we sink below the surface, the buoy we blindly seek to grasp could turn out to be an anchor.

I ate. In order to remove myself from those moments that seemed unbearable, I sought the comforts of macaroni and cheese, heavily sauced pizza and overprocessed fast food. To fill the space within, where I should have been growing a child, I consumed cheesecakes and entire boxes of cookies, scarfed down countless pastries, candies and tubs of ice cream.

I had spent over a year retraining myself to move when I was in a bad place. To get out of my environment and into one where I could run and see the glow of sun or moon on the curve of the road, feel the coolness of wind or rain upon my skin. But I was forbidden from that release. And so I shrouded myself in fleece blankets instead, and I scattered chocolate bar wrappers like petals across the dark table and onto the floor. I stared at the flickering pictures on my television from under half-closed lids, often stretching out on the sofa to surrender to tears, and then sleep.

EVENTUALLY, THE MEDICAL PROFESSIONALS WHO HAD BEEN MONitoring my reproductive health were satisfied with my test results and gave me permission to return to my normal routine, and it was only a short while before the next pregnancy test came back positive. This time our elation was traced with trepidation, but we gave ourselves permission to be hopeful. That hope died when the blood returned.

A second ectopic. A second round of drugs. A second surgery, this one taking my right Fallopian tube. A second baby lost. And then, eight months after making the decision to start a family, a third.

I WAS DRAWN BENEATH THE CURRENT AGAIN. SHOVED BENEATH the surface of self-sabotage. I treaded water with hands curled around thickly iced cakes and fistfuls of greasy potato chips. Over time, I was released again—and then again—from my obligations to follow medically advised exercise sabbaticals. But by then I had allowed old habits to re-establish their deep roots, and I was already teetering on the edge between overweight and obese.

The years that followed sent me deep into the realm of infertility, and with every disappointment, each anxiety over an upcoming appointment or treatment, came the drive to overeat. The pounds I added were a wall of defence against the pain I still felt inside. They were insulation against my fear.

By the time our reproductive treatments proved successful, I had gained back most of the original weight I had lost. And while the pregnancy turned out to be a healthy one that would result in a beautiful, strong son, I found myself unravelling—first as hypervigilance became my solution to anxieties around that pregnancy potentially failing, and then as the earliest months of motherhood stripped away opportunities for independence, self-care and sleep.

I continued in that pattern until my son was about to turn one, six months after my own fortieth birthday. It was those significant milestones, coupled with the reignition of my passion for the written word, that prompted a disengagement from the headspace I had so long occupied.

I began to take a hard look at who I was and, more importantly, at who I wanted to become. And the thing about looking with truly open eyes is that we can be rewarded with unexpected insights.

I am not the number on my scale. I am not the roll of fat that gathers above the waistline of my plus-sized jeans each time I take a seat. I am not defined by my stretch marks, the way the skin hangs from my upper arms, or the double chin I attempt to tilt out of frame for photographs. Likewise, when I lost weight, my character was not determined by the muscles in my back or the leanness of my calves. I did not become a more impressive human being just because I was able to lose over a hundred pounds.

And I am not a failure as a mother because I lost my babies.

That has been the hardest lesson of all. The most difficult insight to believe. But with it comes the story of all that I am.

I am a fighter. I am a fierce and loyal woman who physically, mentally and spiritually lost and regained half of myself on my journey to motherhood. I persevered through trials and found meaning and a purpose for my life. I am now more compassionate and better equipped to help myself and others.

I have learned to be more than a simple caricature, more than a person who is defined only as someone who lost weight or gained it back, who struggled with infertility or became a mom. The truth is vastly richer than those convenient labels might suggest. And I like that about my story—the paradoxes are the stones upon which I hoist my considerable, yet resilient, body, as I climb closer to understanding the scope, nuance and significance of my experiences.

B-WORDS AND F-WORDS: SAFETY, SEX AND THE CIRCLE

Caroline Many

---

*"And in a culture that hates fat women, telling a fat woman she is
beautiful means putting her in a state of cognitive dissonance."*

THE DISTANCE BETWEEN ME AND THE WORLD HAS ALWAYS BEEN
marked in concentric coils. At the inner core lay a perfect circle, the
trusted world, a gravitational centre bounded by the limits of the
farm I grew up on—just me and my family and our animals.

Beyond the circle were overlapping elliptical rings. The first ring
included neighbour friends. In the next, adventure.

Just a few miles away from our farm was the lake where people
from the city and the county would come to spend their summers.
As kids, we helped each other learn the delicate lakeside arts: of
avoiding the beaches with the worst duck mites, of perfectly toasting
marshmallows golden brown over a campfire, of exchanging the best
treats from the canteen with orange two-dollar bills from Mom. We
spent our summers in wet swimsuits and muddied jelly shoes. Sun-
dappled and doped on sugar, our bodies were playgrounds, plush
little pleasure domes. It seemed like one or all of us were always
in some state of undress, yet our nakedness was covert—somehow
always on display but never truly in view.

A few years passed, and the map was drawn a little wider, bound
up in the endless loop of School Bus #38. I lived sixteen kilometres
from the village where high school kids would play hockey and

celebrate their wins and losses with parties in the bush and make-out sessions in their Ford F-150s. In the early 1990s, the uniform was Wranglers, cowboy boots and band shirts for boys; Wranglers, Roper boots and spaghetti-strap tops for girls. On the bus, the boys munched chewing tobacco like cud and spit the remnants into glass Arizona iced tea bottles they carried with them to class. The girls with boyfriends or early morning farm chores or basketball practice would be picked up and driven to school. The rest of us would ride on the bus, gossiping about teachers or playing cards or practising cat's cradle. By junior high, most of the bus riders were boys.

These were the boys who stole my report card and made fun of my As and my teacher's fawning comments. Boys who let me know the surplus of my post-pubescent body was unacceptable by breaking out into a mocking chorus of *Baby Got Back* when I walked past them.

But not all boys. I remember Justin and his flax-coloured hair. Or maybe it was honey. But it was certainly a beautiful not-blond, not-brown colour. In the front there was a wave to it that I suspected was a pesky childhood cowlick he learned to tame in his teen years.

Like me, he was also fifteen and loved playing in the Alberta College honour band, but maybe a bit ironically, if we knew what that meant. Sure, we were both a bit geeky, but at least we got to hang out at the back of the orchestra and hit things with sticks when the score required it. At least we weren't up in the front with those violin prodigy stress cases, stuck in a never-ending competition for first-chair status.

Justin was cool in a way the Wrangler-wearing, cud-chewing boys at school would never learn to be. Probably because he existed in the farthest ring of my expanding social world: the city.

I felt the little feelings stirring and fanned those little embers of hope. Sure, I was chubby or maybe even a little fat, but there was more to me than that. Maybe he saw that I could be an exception.

Maybe he saw that I was smart and a bit more curious than and different from my peers in a way that maybe wasn't a bad thing anymore.

One orchestra practice leading up to our year-end concert, while the conductor was gently berating the horns section, we traded stories about the dorks we went to school with. I was sharing an anecdote about a redneck I had levelled a particularly good insult at. I thought it would make him laugh. And it did. It felt like the sun on my face to see his blue eyes smile and the wavy forelock jiggle as he laughed along with me.

And then he said it.

"Wow. It seems like you really ... threw your weight around."

A thousand embers snuffed in a single sentence. I felt the circle around me draw tighter, closer, narrower to my quivering, 215-pound body—a body I desperately cajoled not to let loose one of the hot wet tears that threatened to spill down my shirt.

Justin was no longer part of my trusted world. He was not even in orbit anymore.

INSIDE THIS CIRCLE, I WAS SAFE. INSIDE, I SET THE RULES: YEAH, I was fat, but kind of cool and maybe worth knowing. I knew who was okay with that, who belonged and could be trusted in the circle. Outside, there was ambiguity and uncertainty.

I did not return to the orchestra after that year. Instead I got a car, a part-time job and freedom, and a plan to be someone else, somewhere else. When I moved four provinces away to go to university in Ottawa, I had to redraw the circle of my trusted world again. I looked for places of safety and familiarity.

When I first arrived, I drove the city endlessly, using mnemonic devices to guide my way through the colonially named streets and avenues.

This did not help. I did not find my people there. They did not live along the boulevards. My people were online. The late nineties might have been the very embryonic days of online meet-up culture, but my people were already there, in chat rooms like Alamak, which had a dedicated following in the Ottawa cyber scene. I was there too, soaking up what we sometimes called the noosphere. I liked that word. The pronunciation of it—no-oh-sphere—was exactly difficult enough to bar entry to anyone who didn't get it, couldn't see the potential for connecting with other people online.

But we were all barely adults. Mostly the rooms were places for the horny, curious and shy to suss each other out before meeting somewhere dark and neutral. I may not have had power over what my body looked like, but there was a different power, a control, to be able to choose how I presented myself in this new, cyber circle.

It required bravery. A lot of bravery. But bravery was the price I was willing to pay for what I wanted: freedom to be myself, to be seen, to connect with others and to be accepted. But if freedom was born of safety, and safety was born of certainty, certainty could come only from full disclosure and good descriptions of what I really looked like.

And that's why there was never a dispute or question in my mind. I would not trick someone into thinking I was thin. I would just be as fat as I was at nineteen. Or as fat as I wasn't. My body continued to change—softening and firming up and expanding seemingly at random.

My face is round, sort of like Kate Winslet's, I would say. My hair is red, like hers was in *Titanic*. Then they would press for more. They would sometimes want measurements, my bra size or my weight. I would offer a neutral adjective instead. Maybe a mildly positive one that didn't sound like it came from the lips of a well-meaning perimenopausal aunt.

Never *Rubenesque* or *zaftig* or, fuck, *pleasantly plump*. Even back then, BBW was mostly used as a dog whistle for porn bodies that didn't look like mine at all. *Plus-sized* hadn't yet entered the lexicon. Calling myself *fat* would make me seem like I hated myself. Worse, it might empower a crush to use it against me at some point. Saying *fat* was not allowed; it might cause the circle to collapse in on itself. *Curvy*. That's what my body is like, I would say. It is *curvy*.

Comparisons were the hardest. There were relatively few young women in Hollywood my size (which fluctuated between 12 and 18). The ones that existed were not always flattering or well-known enough to really be meaningful. Disclosure became easier later, when we figured out how to digitize images and pictures could be emailed after trust was established with a few Alamak chat sessions.

I never met them alone. My friend Jenn and I would round up some other single women and have them round up some of their Alamak crushes so we could go play pool or listen to a terrible band at an Irish pub in the ByWard Market together. If we got messy there would be close conversations in back corners and dares to sneak the best fancy Belgian beer glasses out in our purses before we snickered and staggered into cabs to take us home for make-out sessions that would leave us dry-mouthed and craving cigarettes.

That's how I met Kade, a gargantuan green-eyed ginger with a cute smile. Kade played basketball and listened to rap and smoked weed with his buddies in neighbourhoods that Jenn warned me about. One night we ate cheesecake in a booth at a faux fifties diner, part of a chain that Celine Dion founded. That's where he said it.

Kade called me beautiful in a way I did not believe but that still burned my cheeks with embarrassment. He had told me he thought I was pretty over chat before, but it was late at night and I was sure he was partying with his basketball buddies and it didn't mean anything. This time it was for real. I looked down at the cheesecake and then up at a framed photo of a taut-faced, smiling Celine.

It felt like a terrible thing for him to have to say in order to kiss me. I have never believed the lie of *beautiful*, but now I allow it. Men sometimes feel the need to tell me before we have sex. They say it like it is the first time I've heard those words spoken to me.

Didn't Kade know? *Beautiful* did not belong to a fat body with flabby arms and a soft tummy and a chubby face. *Cute*. *Cute* was acceptable inside the circle. *Cute* belonged. *Beautiful* was not the word to use when you wanted to get naked and share bodies. That was *sexy*.

Beautiful is different. It is objectifying and powerful in a way that shames lesser descriptors. Being beautiful isn't just about being desired; it's about being seen, appreciated and understood. Neither *hot* nor *sexy* nor *cute* nor *pretty* can compete. Because *beautiful*? It can't be bought. Not even earned. It is bestowed on you. It doesn't easily shift with the winds of taste culture. And in a culture that hates fat women, telling a fat woman she is *beautiful* means putting her in a state of cognitive dissonance.

Because *beautiful* cannot be argued with. That's why, when wielded by the mouth of a careless man, *beautiful* is a chainsaw, able to mow down defences and separate a woman from her selfhood.

There is no equivalent word a woman can say to a man that carries the same emotional weight. Men can be *sexy* or *cute*. They can certainly be *handsome*. But those words don't work the same way as *beautiful*. If *beautiful* is a wine glass dipped in a well of poisonous promise, *handsome* is a shot glass dusted with a half dose of Viagra.

But Kade didn't know. He was too young, still. After he said that word to me, he looked me dead in the eye and kissed me. I let his tongue find mine. Blue lightning arced between my closed eyes, and my panties got wetter and warmer. We were soon asked to leave for taking things beyond the limits of PG.

On the way out, we passed by another framed photo of less happy-looking Ms. Dion. My mind darted away from the bouncer and back to Canada's sweetheart: Was she shaming me? I'm sorry, Celine— but he really wants to see me naked and it's making me nervous.

Celine might not have approved of the PDA, but I had sex with Kade that night, and he slept over. It was my first time all the way, and it felt really good. I kept the lights off and made sure he couldn't see too much of me. Waking naked together, I remember the sight of our frizzy ginger mounds and freckled arms blending together like some Irish purist's wet dream.

NEARLY TWENTY YEARS LATER, UNDER VERY DIFFERENT CIRCUM-stances, I allowed Shaun to say that same upsetting word to me. Shaun and I had been chatting on Bumble for a week before we met on a late-August Sunday. He arrived at the pub exactly on time and exactly the dark-haired, dimple-cheeked giant—six foot five, give or take—his profile made him out to be.

I didn't stand to greet him but instead stretched upward on my bar stool to give him a hug. I was relaxed in my body, warmed up by hours of patio conversation with other women writers earlier in the day. My mood was as breezy as my outfit—flowy elephant-print pants and a vintage lacy crop top, capped off with a pair of oversized, hexagonal, turquoise sunglasses. I recall the distinct pleasure of rewarding my soft belly with the unfamiliar sensation of sunshine on skin all afternoon.

Shaun seemed at ease. He was new at Bumble but good at it, this online dating thing. Maybe not as good at I was, but I was both an early adopter and a recent convert with scores of first dates in my newly single life.

We talked about the things you do on a first date. He flirted. I flirted back. He shared the cute childhood stories I expected him to. He flatteringly compared me with recent flaky dates. He flaunted his beer-empire family connections. He told me all about working as a TV producer. He unsubtly hinted that he was wealthy.

An hour and a half into our conversation, Shaun gave me that look, and then he said that word: *beautiful.*

Maybe it was the gin. Maybe it was the sun. Maybe it was the crop top. But that day I did not laugh or brush it off. I was not shocked or offended. Not by the word. And not by all the too-fast confirmations of desire.

I smiled and said thank you.

I stepped outside for a cigarette, and when he joined me, I let him do the things I secretly crave. He took my hand in his. He leaned down to kiss me. He put his lanky arm around me. When I had my fill, I told him it was time for me to go to sleep and for him to go home.

Upon his firm insistence, I let him drive me home. It was only a dozen blocks. The bus would be a forty-minute wait. And, I worried, saying no might not be something he would entertain; I could not throw my weight around with this giant.

Soon, we were outside my apartment building. I told him I had to smoke again. He swung around the passenger door to open it. I puffed away.

He insisted he come up. I told him no and changed the subject to my love of aquafit, joking about my physical prowess and my desperate need to wake up at 5:40 the next morning for the pool.

He told me he works out. He said he wanted to show me. Before I could respond, he grabbed me around my thirty-five-inch waist. He lifted all 215 pounds of me straight into the air, his eyes locked on mine. He held me aloft in a bear hug. I gasped. Shock. Disgust. Confusion. Did he not see those flickering across my face?

Maybe.

"Put me down. I'm fat."

We were both surprised by my words. He placed my feet back on the ground. Did he not know the rules? *Beautiful* did not negate my fatness, my safety, my power.

Soon I was back in my apartment. In bed. Asleep. At the pool. Dealing with Monday. Only when I relayed details to my writerly friends did the bizarreness of our goodbye set in.

"How did it go? Was Shaun nice? Hot? Smart? Charming?"

I struggled to find the words to describe the experience. I decided against trying to explain how Shaun had transgressed the circle of the trusted world by calling me beautiful. That his behaviour was only possible in a world without a protective ring of safety and certainty and fatness. But it was too revealing, too convoluted a metaphor. Instead, I said, "He treated me like a thin woman. Like someone accustomed to flattery and expecting dominance. Like someone who's able to brush both those things away."

The silence that followed was a crowd-sourced alarm bell—the kind of sense-making activity that invites more detail and reflection.

This was not normal, they said. This did not happen to them. Not even to my thinnest friends. The pretty ones. The ones who could attract romance from a man as easily as lust. No. Not often. Maybe not ever. It didn't happen.

I didn't know. I thought it was just part of the pantheon of romantic experiences beyond my reach, experiences that exist outside the circle and beyond the promise of a well-written description on a screen. Maybe, if I suspended my boundaries for just a moment, I could walk a little deeper into this unmediated world, where exploring the rites of female romantic passage would finally be possible.

Of having a stranger buy you a drink at a bar. Of getting flowers before a date instead of only after a fight. Of happily accepting a man's claim that you are beautiful. Of not questioning the romantic gestures of someone you haven't first vetted online for their interest in you. Of all the things I imagined thin women must have become accustomed to that I never fully experienced and couldn't comprehend beyond a girlish fantasy fixed in my mind.

I did not account for the fear that thin women likely experience. The worry that maybe they couldn't outrun those long male legs. Maybe they couldn't push away the oversized hand as it reaches down their pants or up their shirt.

Maybe my fatness can't inoculate me from physical danger, either. But perhaps it could buffer the emotional risk that comes with online dating. Because despite my broken ignorance, in my circle I am still a sexualized fat girl. I have been since the first time I heard Sir Mix-a-Lot lyrics barked at me at thirteen. I will be the next time I hear them cooed at me lovingly by a date—one I will definitely have met online.

STRANGER WORDS

Shadoe Ball

"I used to feel so alone in my fat body. Now I feel as though we are on the precipice of a fat revolution."

QUESTION: DOES IT HURT MORE WHEN A FAMILY MEMBER MAKES a negative comment about your body or when a stranger does?

This was asked at a focus group I recently attended about living in a big body. Many of the participants felt that it hurt more coming from family members. The group then proceeded to share stories that simultaneously interwove sadness, shock and humour. We nodded in agreement, anguish and awe.

But the more I think about it, the more I realize that the opposite was true for me. I've let comments from strangers impact me so much more than anything a family member has said. Luckily, I come from a big family (both types of big: lots of people but also size of individuals), so it was always easy to jab back. Good-heartedly. In a way that eases pain and shares a laugh.

Yet, in public, I must keep composure. It's more than wanting to keep my cool. I also want to make sure I don't add fuel to the "fat bitch" stereotype. So what do I do? I ignore it and move on with my day. The path of least resistance is my way.

However, what really happens? I am "off" for the rest of the week. Quieter. Clumsy. I am stuck in my own thoughts again. Not able to stay in the present moment. My whole life I have yearned to fit in.

I put on the role of rebellious, blunt, loud fat lady as a teen—with sharp, sarcastic lines that I would bring out whenever necessary. I put on the role of sweet, caring, bubbly fat lady in my twenties. Excusing my body. Excusing my presence. Constantly thinking about how I appear to others. Investing much more time each morning to put on my armour.

Armour Strategy 101

STEP 1: WEAR THE "KIND FATTY" UNIFORM: A FLORAL WRAP DRESS with sensible but feminine shoes. Glasses. Pulled back hair. Tiny earrings. Small purse. Ensuring I minimize any part of myself that is controllable.

Step 2: Pick out the book I will read on transit. While I enjoy reading, the book itself is not important. It is more of a security blanket sometimes. A signal for my intelligence. A way to ignore the glares of others without appearing rude.

Step 3: Once in public, make sure others always have the right-of-way.

THE ARMOUR IS USEFUL. I THINK EACH PERSON HAS THEIR OWN version of the armour. Some people use negative comments about others to superficially strengthen their armour. When I tell my friends that a stranger has called me fat, they rush to say, "But you're not that fat!" as if there were some line where if I was "that" fat, it would be okay for the stranger to act callously.

The most recent time this happened was last fall. I was walking into the Bathurst subway station at 2:00 p.m. on a Tuesday. A calm vibe settles over the city at that time of day. The perfect time to get to a doctor's appointment in East York. I was contemplating how lovely the east end of the city really is and considering where I might go following my appointment. I was having a great day, and then it happened.

I was walking down the stairs as a stranger made eye contact with me going up the escalator. I smiled at them. They proceeded to look me up and down and say, "You should probably lose some weight."

I just kept walking, startled but not surprised. This happens semi-regularly to me. About three times per year someone I have never met sees me and feels compelled to make a comment about my body.

If you've ever felt compelled to point out someone's physicality, please resist. Now, I must admit that I am guilty of this: I always feel compelled to ask tall people how tall they are. Once, I was simply standing beside a tall person on the subway and was trying to low-key look at how tall he was by looking at our reflections. Well, he caught me and whispered, "Six foot seven." I was incredibly embarrassed.

Another time, I was out with a friend and had recently lost a noticeable amount of weight. My friend made a big deal about how much better (i.e., thinner) I looked, and then we had a nice dinner. When my friend went to the bathroom, a stranger came up to me and said, "Wow, you must have been a real heifer if she is saying you look good now."

He left, my friend returned from the bathroom, and I didn't tell her—because I didn't want to ruin our nice evening. We walked to the bus stop, hugged and parted ways. I cried on the way home.

What both examples spotlight for me is that I cannot simply exist. No matter how large I am, people notice my body. Just like I noticed the tall man. I want to strengthen my armour. If only I had a quip like "Six foot seven."

Then, through different forms of therapy, it was shown to me that I can build my armour from within.

It started with a poem:

I no longer want to yell "I am NOT" when someone tells me I'm fat.
I want to pity them, for they lack knowledge.
They do not understand what it is like to move through the world in
*   a body deemed worthy of mentioning upon sight.*
I want to pity them, for they lack knowledge.
They have not learned that attempting to humiliate a stranger only
*   makes them look foolish.*
I want to pity them, yet,
I also envy them,
For these very same reasons.
Additional knowledge adds additional complexity.
To the understanding of your own world.
To the understanding of others.
This complexity brings on anxiety.
An anxiety that has silenced me.
When I was young,
My most prized possession
Was a caustic tongue.
A defence mechanism.
Ready to deploy at any time.
Mutually assured destruction was on my mind all the time.
Did you notice my body?
Enough to mention it?
Get ready to feel the fire, you piece of shit.
But this doesn't improve things, does it?
It made me feel better,
But just like whisky,
Playing with this fire was risky.
The words burned my throat on the way out and in my gut when idle.
Is there a way to turn down the heat?
Surely, I can exist without feeling like a cheat?
Must I wear armour every day?

Just let me live,
Or get out of my way!

This poem has helped me feel a lot better. When I go out in public, I think about it. How lucky I am to understand that most people do not want their body pointed out, and that not everyone has this knowledge. It's comforting.

A FEW WEEKS FOLLOWING THE INCIDENT AT BATHURST STATION, I had to return. I was feeling confident that day, and, instead of having a book to read on the bus, I had brought a book to sketch in instead. I'd picked up a new set of pens that morning that I was itching to try out. I was thinking about the incident, pretty sure it wasn't going to happen again but fully armoured in case, and then I wrote down the word *Fat*. In big, loopy letters. The fresh ink was gliding so nicely along the notebook that I felt inspired to doodle a small flower on the tip of the *t*. I then covered the entire word with these small, simple flowers, alternating between colours, absorbed in my own world. When I was close to my stop I made eye contact with a stranger again. We were approaching the station and I was putting the book away.

But I caught something different in the eye of this stranger. Instead of disgust at my body, there was curiosity about what I had been doing. She smiled at me. I smiled back. A moment of kindness I will always remember.

That night, I started my Instagram account, The Word Fat. Each week, I post a few images that I've created using the word *fat* as inspiration. This makes me more mindful in my daily activities as I am always seeking a new, fresh background to use.

This account has also changed how my brain interprets my reflection. My feed for this account has been carefully curated. Following the hashtags #fat, #fatty, #fatart, #fatartists, #fatbodies, etc., I have had my eyes opened to a world of representation. I can look in the mirror, with an expanded lens on what beautiful is, and it helps.

Beyond beauty, there is simply a validating element to all of this. I used to feel so alone in my fat body. Now I feel as though we are on the precipice of a fat revolution. It has been exhilarating to see bodies like mine in poses, clothing and environments I thought were accessible only to thinner people. Accessible to me if I lost "enough" weight. And, from what I have seen in my thirty-two years, it's never going to be "enough."

So what is more painful? A negative comment from your family or from a stranger? Maybe it doesn't matter? I am not sure.

I am only sure that I can work on my own armour. It can be softened in spots and strengthened in others. Perhaps I can work on my swords too. I have kept them hidden for a while. They will be helpful in the revolution.

NAVIGATING RADICAL SELF-LOVE AND BODY NEUTRALITY

Amanda Scriver

"Whether you realize it or not, diet culture has warped us. It has taught us what types of bodies are acceptable in society."

THIS BODY OF MINE, WE'VE BEEN ON AN EPIC JOURNEY TOGETHER. We've been through some good times and some bad times. We've had some high times and some low times. But through it all, my body has changed in ways I never thought possible. In my eyes, my body is the best she's ever looked or felt—internally and externally.

I am a fat woman; I have no shame in admitting that. I have rolls and a double chin. My skin is soft and pliable. I do not have a thigh gap, although media everywhere keep telling me that I need one. I have skin dimples in places you'd likely never expect and scars from a skin disease I'm still embarrassed to talk about. But with all that said, I am not ashamed of this body or who I am. My body is a gift to this world, and quite frankly I don't give a fuck what any of the trolls on the internet or people staring at me on the subway think.

But I won't lie to you. I can't say it's been an easy journey—rather, quite the opposite. Learning to love yourself regardless of your size is one of the most crucial and beneficial gifts you can give to yourself. But my path to self-love and self-acceptance has had every curve and bump—and it started off with a lot of self-hate and self-destruction.

LIKE A TREE PLANTING ITS ROOTS DEEP INSIDE THE GROUND, MY mom planted self-doubt in me. She taught me to be ashamed of myself. She taught me that my body was a currency I could exchange for social worth. She taught me that I couldn't be happy until I restricted myself, informing me about all the diets I could try. I learned from her all the worst behaviours and, because of her, I was never happy with myself.

I tried SlimFast shakes and signed up for Weight Watchers. I tracked my meals in a notebook, eating as many foods as possible that had zero points. I tried to restrict myself as much as I possibly could because I believed that if I were skinnier, I would be valued and wanted. I thought being fat meant I had failed both myself and others around me. I thought being fat meant that no one would desire me or hire me, and that it was my only identifier. I didn't understand that this behaviour was both destructive and harmful.

From the time I was very young, diet culture had waged its war on my thoughts and my body. It had attacked everything around me, from my character to my own eating habits. I thought constantly about how I could lose weight, even once considering if a jar of baby food was an acceptable meal replacement to help me lose weight faster. I never did it (thank God) but I did try every fad diet and eat every "low-carb" or "weight-loss-friendly" meal you can imagine.

Week after week, I would weigh myself in to my Weight Watchers group, but not much would change. Ten pounds lost here, fifteen pounds gained there, and many tears in solitude. Food had finally lost all meaning for me. It was never just eating; it was about valuing what foods were "good" or "bad" for me and how I could attain this unattainable and unhealthy goal of being skinny.

I DIDN'T KNOW WHAT FATPHOBIA WAS. I NEVER UNDERSTOOD HOW much rage, disgust and emotional warfare my fat body provoked in others. Without even knowing it, I had grown up with fatphobia all around me. The people who were supposed to be my biggest supporters in life were the ones who were the most fatphobic. It was chipping away at my confidence. I didn't know that I could escape, but I did know this: it was like being suffocated.

Whether you realize it or not, diet culture has warped us. It has taught us what types of bodies are acceptable in society and it has told us we aren't valued unless we are thin. Diet culture creates an environment where we are expected to second-guess some of our most basic and intuitive desires, which sets us up to second-guess many other parts of our lives. It has created a system that demonizes and hates fat people, a system that continues to tear down and profit off bodies like mine.

Honestly, fuck that noise.

I remember the day I decided to cut it all out and things started to change. I went to my weekly Weight Watchers appointment after nearly starving myself and working out three times that week. Our leader asked me to step up onto the scale; I had gained five pounds. I was so angry. She looked at me and said, "Maybe you're just not recording things properly?" At this point, I was barely eating three meals a day.

I felt a blackout rage go through me, different from anything I had ever felt before. I wanted to burn that entire building down. But then I realized: I didn't need this shit. I was so tired and exhausted. I knew that I needed to eliminate the negative forces from my life, but how? Everything was so ingrained.

How to get off this hamster wheel, exactly?

IN 2009 I LOGGED IN TO TUMBLR FOR THE FIRST TIME AND CAME across the blog *Fuck Yeah, Fat Positive*. It was radical and touted itself as a fat-positive space where no discussions of dieting would be had. I had never heard of such a thing and was shocked that such a space existed.

I scrolled endlessly through the images of beautiful bodies just like mine. They were fat, happy and proud of who they were, spreading messages that were honest and positive. I had never encountered anything like this, and it was everything I needed at that moment. I cried.

Maybe I was naive, but it was hard to believe that people like me existed out there and that communities like this existed and were thriving. For once in my life, I found a place where my body felt accepted. It became a home away from home, but it also became an awakening. Immediately, I sought out more and more images of folks who looked like me.

THE WORLDS OF FAT POSITIVITY AND BODY ACCEPTANCE WERE concepts that were totally new and foreign to me. As I learned more, I knew I wanted to become a part of this movement. I threw myself into the body positivity movement in 2013 and decided I needed to really dig deep into myself.

Through this movement, I learned that fat bodies like mine were valid. That my body was my choice and I was worthy of respect, no matter how my body looked. I learned that I was the most powerful person in my life and that it was okay to accept myself and love myself just the way I was. I had never had anyone tell me this my entire life and, honestly, just hearing it was revolutionary.

But the body positivity movement as I discovered it was changing and becoming mainstream. Just about everywhere I turned, for better and for worse, people were shouting about being body positive. Hell, beauty brand Dove wanted me to be more positive about my body, and I really didn't know what to think about it.

In reality, this wasn't a bad thing. But for so long, society had deemed fat folks unacceptable and cast us aside. When conventionally thin or fit people were hopping into the body-positive space and putting down roots in the fat-acceptance movement, I got mad.

For fat folks, our fight is never over. Our bodies will always be undermined or viewed as physically, economically or emotionally unnecessary. Take a quick glance through the #bodypositive or #bopo hashtags on Instagram, and you'll find plenty of images of mostly thin, white women usually slouched over to fake the appearance of rolls. Isn't this the exact opposite of what the body positivity movement is supposed to be about?

It has been exhausting and upsetting for me, as I can't hide my fat body. It's always on display and visible for others to openly mock and deem "unhealthy." Listen, I get it: body positivity is a movement focused on shining the spotlight onto marginalized bodies, and I'm all about people of all shapes and sizes sharing their sexy selves and feeling empowered online. But I cannot ignore the erasure of fat bodies from the body positivity movement online and offline.

Where does this leave us and the relationships we are navigating with our bodies? There is so much trauma and pain tied up in our bodies and trying to figure out what exactly body love means to us. This is why navigating something like body positivity, as I quickly found out, can't solve the messy and complicated trauma history that so many people have with their bodies. This is how I discovered radical self-love and self-acceptance.

AS I BEGAN TO NAVIGATE EXACTLY WHAT RADICAL SELF-LOVE AND self-acceptance meant for me, I tried to find spaces that affirmed and celebrated different kinds of bodies. For so long, my body had been rendered invisible or invalid in contemporary spaces because my fat body wasn't allowed to take up space. But for the first time, I found love in one of the most unlikely places of all: a room, naked, with a handful of other women.

The class was called Body Pride and was taught by a sex educator in Toronto. I mentioned it to some friends, but no one was quite as interested as I was. While I didn't quite know what to expect from the session, I decided to throw caution to the wind and sign up anyway, all by myself. I figured I had nothing to lose, and at this point, I was willing to do anything to make myself feel less self-conscious about my own body.

I arrived at the building where the workshop was being held and took a deep breath. I was greeted by the instructor and shown into the room with eight other women. The goal of the session was to teach each of us how to desexualize nudity and also how to learn to accept our bodies, all while completely naked.

In society, we're told that in order to be considered beautiful or desirable, we must conform or fit into beauty standards. As I sat in this circle of women, who came from a wide variety of backgrounds (including weights, ages, abilities and race), one thing was abundantly clear: we were all experiencing the same thoughts, feelings and anxieties.

All humans struggle with body self-love and acceptance. While it may seem scary or uncomfortable at first to be naked, when you're faced with strangers, you begin to realize your imperfections are really not that imperfect after all. Being able to sit face to face with others experiencing the same internal and emotional struggles was huge for me.

But it was also my first step toward looking at my body with love—and the first time I pulled at the strings of my trauma and my relationship with my body. I had never quite understood just how interconnected they were. It is an everyday struggle that I'm still learning to navigate. I don't have all the answers yet.

TODAY I PRACTISE SOMETHING CALLED BODY NEUTRALITY, WHICH is a far cry from where I was ten years ago when I first read those Tumblr blogs. Body neutrality is rooted in acknowledging what your body does, not how it appears.

Something I've learned is this: your body is essential to you, and you only get one. Your body's well-being is entwined with your overall well-being. So how can we stop hating our body? Give it time and give it space. Allow your body the time to breathe, and lean into the fact that being positive about your body is not always realistic. Your body is beautiful and badass. But so often, we don't listen to it.

Today, I want you to start listening to it—listening to the trauma within. Different people handle this in different ways, and that's okay. Everybody's body journey is going to be different, and it's not a race to the end. What matters and what is important is that we stop silently judging ourselves, and others, and learn to be a little more fat and abundant—flaws and all.

FOR THE LOVE OF SASQUATCH

Katy Weicker

"They praise the rapidly downward plunge on the scale. They affirm what I've always suspected: that thin is beautiful."

I AM SEVEN. I SIT ON THE STEPS OF THE SCHOOL, A CUPCAKE IN hand. My mouth waters as I stare at the whipped chocolate frosting.

"Hey, Sasquatch!" a voice booms.

Carefully, meticulously, I peel the wax-paper wrapper away from the moist, fudgy dessert. Flecks of chocolate snow fall onto my navy-blue uniform. I lick my finger, press it to the crumbs, collecting them like precious gold nuggets.

"Sasquatch!" the voice shouts again, this time more pointedly. I glance up. A few feet away, the new kid, a boy with frizzy ginger curls and liver-spot freckles, is grinning at me. My deeply engrained politeness tells me I should smile back, but something about him makes my insides shiver. His grin is torqued like a creepy clown mask as he tips his chin in my direction, his eyes locked on mine. I squirm as he puffs out his cheeks and pushes up his nose with his middle finger. "Sasquatch!"

An indignant tightness swells in my chest.

"Get lost, Carrots!" I holler. His peach skin turns red under his tan freckles as he glowers at me. I feel proud and rebellious (and a little shameful) at my comeback.

"Fatty!" he cackles before sprinting toward the playground.

My smugness dissipates as I stare down at the treat in my chubby hands. The moniker Sasquatch rings in my ears. I shove the entire cupcake into my gullet. It pours into the crevasses of my chipmunk cheeks, smoothing the creases of my dimples into round orbs of baby fat. I can't breathe. I mash it against the roof of my mouth, creating a pasty ball of mush, which I quickly swallow. It tugs at my esophagus, choking me as it slips into my stomach, my dirty secret devoured by shame.

I AM IN GRADE FOUR. OUR TEACHER, A ROBUST, GREY-HAIRED woman who wears floral polyester pantsuits and smells like an elevator of grandmothers, announces we are going to make "Wanted" posters naming ourselves as outlaws (Catholic schools must come up with creative ways to indoctrinate deep-seated guilt from an early age). She hands out grainy, photocopied eight-by-ten templates with a square in which we are to crudely sketch self-portraits. Our renegade sins will be listed below our pictures, along with our vital stats. I tap the eraser of my pencil against my desk, chew my lip and allow my imagination to soar.

Carefully, meticulously, I craft my story. I am a horse thief. I have stolen a palomino who was beaten by his cruel owner because he could not run as fast as the others. Together, we rob monocle-wearing fat cats and give their riches to misfits and outcasts. When my tale of bravery is complete, I turn to my portrait, laboriously drawing a beautiful face, erasing the left eye because it's bigger than the right, crafting a jawline and shading cheekbones into an exquisite creature. When I'm done, I look down at the space below. *Age: nine. Height: (mental note to check with Mom). Weight ...*

I crumple the paper. My fingers ache as I squeeze my story into a tiny ball. The next morning, I tell my mom my stomach hurts and spend the day in bed watching *Robin Hood* and eating Kraft Dinner.

I AM FIFTEEN. FINALLY, SOCIETALLY ACCEPTABLE FAT HAS FORMED. Unfortunately, additional rolls have appeared too, reducing the effectiveness of the large mounds weighing heavily on my chest. I have a friend. She has an older brother. He is tall, dark and beautiful. He has a car and a job. He plays the guitar and sings. I love him.

I find excuses to hang out at their house. Carefully, meticulously, I bathe in Gap Dream perfume and Vanilla Fields body spray, cake my mouth in Dr. Pepper–flavoured lip gloss.

One night, we are all sitting on the couch watching a random movie starring Nicolas Cage, me sandwiched awkwardly between the siblings. I crush my elbows into my ribs, in an effort to deepen the crease between my societally acceptable lumps of fat and hide the muffin top spilling over the waist of my jeans.

My friend excuses herself. She mumbles something about needing more pizza or Diet Coke or the toilet; I'm too focused on the fact that her brother's aura is touching mine.

When she leaves, he and I sit in silence, my body humming as I squish it into itself. Out of the corner of my eye, I see his hand move from the bulge in his lap to the back of the couch, his muscular arm reaching around me. His fingers clamp tightly around the soft, pudgy flesh of my bicep. A spike of adrenaline courses through my swollen body. The feeling is foreign; I can't tell if I like it. Either way, I know I'm ashamed of it (Catholic scars run deep).

"If you ever tell anyone about this, I'll deny it," he growls into my ear. The smell of Old Spice and Dippity-Do hair gel overpowers me as he pounces, crushing me into the couch, splaying my fat like an insignificant bug on a windshield. I feel out of control. I'm not sure which is worse: fat or small.

A tiny voice from my past ruthlessly whispers, "Sasquatch."

I push him away.

He scoffs and mutters, "Frigid whore."

I instantly regret rejecting him, but the damage is done. My role has been cast—forever the fat friend. So, I lose. I lose him. I lose control, my identity, my personality. I lose weight, starve myself and struggle to morph into something, anything, other than the girl who is so uncomfortable in her own skin that she would push away a boy she's been lusting after for six months out of fear he might notice her back rolls.

People comment. They comment on how great I look. They praise the rapidly downward plunge on the scale. They affirm what I've always suspected: that thin is beautiful. My mother tells me I'm moody. My body tells me I'm hangry. I step on the scale multiple times a day and panic if the number isn't less than it was the last time. It plummets. I'm starving but satiated.

Rumours begin to fly that my best friend's brother has slept with another one of her friends. I cry. I eat a cookie. I eat again. And again. And again.

I gain.

It doesn't matter anymore.

I AM THIRTY-TWO. I CAN'T WALK UP A FLIGHT OF STAIRS WITHOUT being winded. My body aches, aged beyond its years by the folds of fat crushing it. Carefully, meticulously, I eat entire bags of Doritos, hiding the evidence from the judgmental eyes of my cats, secretly concerned they will gleefully eat my painfully single face if I drop dead of a heart attack. Five ... four ... three ... two ... one ... happy new year. I don't believe in resolutions, but I can't do this anymore. Enough is enough.

I AM THIRTY-THREE. THE TAGS ON MY CLOTHES NO LONGER BEAR A mark of shame. The number on the scale no longer causes my soul to retch. I have shed 111 pounds. I can count my ribs, and calories, and steps, with ease. I've grown to love spaghetti squash and hiking mountains, morphed from morbidly obese to curvy, slayed sugar cravings and fat cells.

Carefully, meticulously, I weigh my food, measure my portions and inches to keep my former body at bay. I pinch my collarbone, run my fingers down the bumps of my spine, grind the heels of my palms against my hip bones, just to make sure I can feel the newly unearthed hardness of my bones. Because, buried in the fibres of my activewear and stretch marks, she's still there. The freak of nature who never belonged, who exists to entice curiosity and live a life of solitude, struggling to remain hidden for fear of disparagement if she's seen.

I meet someone. He is tall, dark and beautiful. He writes poetry and journalism; he listens to songs by men with guitars whose lyrics are deeper than the ocean. He does not know my dirty secret and, despite the words percolating inside me, I bite my lip and refuse to expose it. For the first time, Sasquatch is a myth—even more so, a legend he's never heard. He smiles at me. I smile back. My core shifts along with my universe; I can feel it tilt on its axis. My smile flickers and, despite every encounter in my past telling me I'm misreading the signs, I swear his does too. I can feel the heat exploding in my cheeks. It's awkward. My heart skips. I love him. From a distance, of course, because it's the love I believe I am worthy of.

He takes initiative and my inhibitions begin to ease. We exchange contact information, but I tell myself it's because we work together. Over time I can feel the distance grow shorter—despite my past telling me I'm crazy, I swear I can. We talk daily, exchange stories on paper and text. He tells me his secrets. I don't tell him mine. It is summer. It is hot. I wear long-sleeved shirts and he asks me why. I dodge suggestions of pizza and ice cream, hoping he won't misinterpret this as a lack of interest. We walk on beaches and eat hummus as I struggle to navigate my emotions.

Carefully, meticulously, I stand at night in front of the mirror. When I am alone and the shiny new man has long since been dismissed by a good-night message, I lift my arms to the sides and allow bat wings of skin to flop from my armpits. I allow my breasts to sag, my stomach to flap like an inflated balloon in the wind. I examine the reminder of my past before sitting down at my desk. Carefully, meticulously, I allow Sasquatch's story to bleed onto my computer screen.

I ask him to read my tale. I taste bile and despair as he discovers my secret. Tears prickle at my insecurities as he turns to me. I brace myself for an all-too-familiar rejection because Sasquatch is unlovable. Instead, he takes my face in his hands. He cups my insecurities in his palms, pressing them to his lifeline. He tells me he's proud of me. He respects me. He runs his hands over my pizza-dough belly that only becomes more pliable the more I suck it in. He kisses me. He tells me I'm beautiful and a tiny ember of possibility believes him. I cling to this with white knuckles, even if my past tells me it's crap.

I AM THIRTY-FOUR. I WALK FOR PLEASURE, NOT PUNISHMENT. I eat s'mores on camping trips and try to ignore my grandmother as she clutches for her pearls when I eat a cookie. I eat takeout when I'm too tired to cook, and cake when I celebrate a familial milestone. My love of spaghetti squash has been replaced with a rediscovery of real freaking pasta. The scale shows a number that makes my soul retch, despite my ability to continue to keep more than eighty pounds of my loss at bay. When we take pictures, angles are beginning to matter again, and even when the perfect one is achieved, I'm still unsatisfied. When I run my fingers across my stomach, it moves like Jell-O, and the irony that I miss the pliability of my pizza-dough paunch is not lost on me. When I mourn this, the man I love reminds me I'm beautiful. I still struggle to believe him, but blind faith is better than no faith at all.

I tell myself tomorrow I will reset, that I will win this battle, but tomorrow comes and, despite the tightness in the band of my jeans and the countless articles of single-digit clothing hanging helplessly in my closet, I stumble. But I continue to get up and fight the battle because I owe it to myself to keep going. To remind myself of how far I've come. To honour the past to prevent it from becoming the future.

Though some of the time-faded details of my journey may be twisted remnants of childhood memories, I still tell them over and over to myself. I may have been eating a vanilla cupcake when I was bullied by Carrots; the movie may have starred Bruce Willis the night my friend's brother branded me. I cannot say with certainty that my grade four teacher wore polyester, though I know for a fact that the man I love loves my body even when I cannot.

But there is one thing of which I am positive: Sasquatch is real. She hibernates in the dark, cragged corners of my being. Licking her wounds, struggling to be treasured, to understand her place in the world and to be accepted for the fragile, glorious monster that she is.

TEN THINGS I LOVE ABOUT BEING FAT

Emily Allan

"There is something to be said for unabashed fatphobia as a quick and easy litmus test as to whether or not someone is worth my time."

TWO THOUSAND ONE. THE YEAR BRITNEY SPEARS AND JUSTIN Timberlake took to the red carpet at the American Music Awards in their iconic, matching head-to-toe denim. The year I watched *Miss Congeniality*, *Legally Blonde* and *10 Things I Hate about You* (gifted to me on DVD—a new thrill) on repeat, until I could anticipate every line and ruin the experience for anyone watching with me. The year I kept my Neopets alive and well for a triumphant five-month streak. The year I informed my parents, to their relief, that I no longer liked the Spice Girls (an opinion I have obviously since rescinded). The year I first heard someone say I'd be pretty if I "lost a few pounds."

Ten-year-old me always had pink cheek glitter and at least two Lip Smackers on hand, and butterfly clips in my gelled-back, curly hair—two spiralling strands free to frame the face, of course. That year, I bought my first pair of Dorinhas (if you do not know what these are, I envy you), their extremely low rise ("the original one-inch zipper!") squeezing my belly upward and out like Silly Putty.

Over sticky watermelon Freezies on her lawn one summer day, my best (and very thin) friend casually said to me, "I like you like this. I can't imagine you being skinny." I was mortally offended, embarrassed, ashamed. "Thanks?" I responded after a few moments of tense preteen silence. It took me until about last year to agree with her.

I went from being a relatively small kid to being a solidly pudgy kid over the course of a couple of years, starting when I was about seven. It happened pretty inexplicably—at least, inexplicable to a culture that is in deep denial of the fact that some bodies are just naturally fat. I grew up on a small island in British Columbia, eating meals prepared by a granola-adjacent mother and running around outside a whole lot. My diet didn't change. I was doing the same two activities I had always done.

I just sort of ... puffed out. And I have remained puffed ever since. While the world has treated my body, since that point in time, as the number one thing holding me back from my own happiness, I am finally starting to understand that the opposite is true. There is so much joy to be had because of, not despite, my body. See, existing outside of a realm of acceptability, while challenging and often heart-breaking, also allows for a unique and magical kind of freedom. I am slowly but surely beginning to crack this freedom open and also realize where it has already benefited me throughout my life.

To explain what I mean, I'd like to present you with a list: here are all the things I have come to love about being fat.

1. It saved me from being popular in high school.

OF COURSE, I WOULD HAVE DETESTED THIS NOTION AT THE TIME. High school was the hardest time in my life in terms of my relationship with my body. I looked at my friends (all of whom were straight-sized and many of whom were very thin) with excruciating envy, though I would never let them see it, and I always felt I was not having the kind of teenage years I was supposed to. I had lots of great friends, though, and I wouldn't say I was bullied. During high school in Vancouver, which I have realized is a notoriously polite and passive-aggressive city, most of the fat-shaming I experienced (and there was a lot) was more subtle and insidious than outright.

But I've also realized that, while it wouldn't fit into TNA and American Apparel like it was "meant" to, my fat body saved me from a lot. Though I certainly tried, I always knew I wasn't going to fit the mould of popular femininity. While this brought a lot of pain, it also brought some relief. I felt like I was failing at looking how I was supposed to look anyway, so I focused on things I could succeed at, like being there for my friends, getting good grades, developing my taste in music and thinking of totally sick burns—all things that have shaped who I am and served me well into my adult life. And the biggest blessing of all? None of the popular boys wanted to date me, so I didn't have to deal with them. If that's not an obvious plus, I don't know what is.

2. I am incredibly soft and comfy.

I'M BASICALLY A HUMAN PILLOW! MY PLUMP, PLUSH ROLLS HAVE provided a cozy place of rest and refuge for my best friends and romantic partners over the years. I know this because they've told me, but also because I'll rest my head on myself when position and flexibility permit. Even new friends and acquaintances often tell me I'm a great hugger. It has become a point of pride. If you have never cuddled a fat person, you are truly missing out.

3. At the risk of perpetuating this stereotype: it made me funny.

THOUGH I ALSO GREW UP WITH A CLASSICALLY SHAMELESS "FUNNY dad," I cannot deny the role that being a fat kid played in forming my sense of humour, which continues to be my favourite thing about myself. My getting fat actually coincided with when I started coming out of my shell as a kid. Though I was a pretty classic middle child (read: attention-seeking ham), I was also very shy in groups and around people I didn't know. When my body changed and I couldn't fly under the radar anymore at school, I learned to use humour as a pre-emptive defence mechanism.

When you live in a body people feel entitled to ridicule, you learn pretty quickly how to protect yourself. Defence mechanisms usually get framed as being negative, but I feel this one has always served me well, especially as I grew up and learned to use it in tandem with being emotionally vulnerable with people who are safe for me. Maybe people who know me absolutely disagree and think I should hash this out in therapy. If you are one of these people and you are reading this, feel free to e-transfer me.

4. It keeps me warm through the bitter Toronto winters.

I DON'T KNOW IF THIS ONE IS SCIENTIFICALLY SOUND, AND MY quick Google search did not provide me with a definite answer. Maybe I just run hot for other reasons—correlation does not equal causation and all that. But I truly think having more fat on my body makes the harsh Canadian winter more bearable. And if you live in Canada (other than on the West Coast, which is a jab I can make because I grew up there), you know that "winter" encompasses and eclipses most of the year.

I may be sweatier through the summers, but my thin friends are constantly cold as soon as October hits, and they stay shivering until May or June. This must be so hard, I honestly cannot imagine. I'm genuinely sorry they have to go through that.

5. It delayed my sexual experimentation past when I was most vulnerable.

THE WAY SOCIETY TREATED MY BODY, IN COMBINATION WITH MY pious dedication to my Christian upbringing throughout my youth, meant I wasn't comfortable exploring my sexuality until much later than most of my peers. I spent my early twenties feeling embarrassingly stunted in this arena. To be clear: this was really hard. It contributed to the feelings of undesirability, shame and fear that were already swirled into the complicated relationship I had with my body.

However, when I did start fumbling into my sexuality, I was at a more self-assured place in my life. I knew myself better and knew how to advocate for myself and my boundaries in a way that I personally didn't when everyone around me was starting to have sex. This is, of course, not a comment on anyone else's readiness or maturity at this stage. I also know this is certainly not every fat person's experience; but it was mine, and in retrospect, I'm grateful for it.

6. It has made me an excellent thrift shopper.

OVER THE PAST FEW YEARS, ONE WAY THAT I'VE COME TO LOVE MY body has been through embracing and defining my own style. Of course, as a fat woman this is far from easy—and I'm aware that, at a size 16, I really don't know the half of it. But being too big for most mainstream clothing stores is still a challenge. Fashionable plus-sized clothes are hard to find, and the options that do exist are expensive. Reasonably priced ones tend to have things like excessive ruching, neon lace panels and unnecessary, decorative zippers.

If you hold the privilege of never having thought about this, please go to the Forever21 website and look at the difference in style between their straight-sized and plus-sized lines. Then start looking at the largest sizes available at all of your favourite stores, and think about how many people you know who are bigger than that. Start advocating for us. Style can be so empowering, and so hard to cultivate with limited options.

Luckily, I have discovered that thrift stores (not vintage stores, which tend to have the same size cut-off as the rest of the straight-sized clothing industry, if not smaller, thank you very much) can be absolute gold mines. My being fat has thus forced me to develop a pretty sweet knack for finding gems and has saved me a lot of money.

7. We have Lizzo.

I DON'T FEEL THE NEED TO ELABORATE ON THIS.

8. It gives me a smug sense of superiority in thin spaces.

WHO DOESN'T LIKE FEELING BETTER THAN EVERYONE AROUND them? I'm only partially joking. When you immerse yourself in body positivity and fat liberation, something wild happens: you realize that your body has never actually been the problem, that it is no one's business but yours, and that people's opinions about it are actually about themselves. When I'm in spaces that can easily feel suffocating (artsy-person parties, public pools, indie music shows, shopping malls), I get to feel a little self-righteous thrill that I'm in on this secret that those around me almost certainly are not.

Honestly, sometimes it even slides into pity for those less enlightened. And if I'm with my rad gang of fat friends? Oh, baby, add strength in numbers to the ecstasy of subverting social marginalization and you've got a full-blown fat superiority complex. I'm not saying I'm necessarily proud of this; I'm just saying it feels really, really good.

9. I'm super strong.

EMOTIONALLY AND MENTALLY, SURE, YES, BUT I'M TALKING LITeral physical strength. Most people don't realize this: carrying around weight builds muscle. I'm solid as a rock. Very sturdy. Not easily knocked over. Plus, I'm tall *and* fat. I have been in situations where being a bit physically intimidating either is fun (like protecting my friends from loathsome exes on the dance floor with a move I have dubbed "bootyguarding") or honestly makes me feel safer.

10. It has given me an excellent radar for shallow assholes.

LOOK, I UNDERSTAND THAT WE ALL HAVE FATPHOBIA AND DIET culture running deep in our psyches, and everyone I love (myself included) has lots of unlearning to do. But there is something to be said for unabashed fatphobia as a quick and easy litmus test as to whether or not someone is worth my time. It's great information to have, particularly in the social circles I tend to operate in where people present themselves as progressive.

Fatphobia is a form of discrimination that has yet to really be socially condemned, so even lefty metropolitan millennials mostly don't know yet to hide it in order to be cool. When I'm making a new friend at a party and their eyes keep flitting down disapprovingly to my stomach, on display in a crop top and high-waisted jeans just like everyone else is wearing? I know that is not a new friend at all. When I'm swiping through on dating apps and someone has chosen to include a weight limit for potential partners? Wow, not the one for me! When I'm talking to a self-appointed feminist ally and it becomes clear that his allyship does not extend to women like me whom he doesn't find attractive? A great indicator that he's not an ally and cannot be trusted as one!

Do you see what I'm getting at? Once you get past the fact that you're being treated as less human because of how you look, it can feel like a pretty nifty sixth sense.

SO, THERE YOU HAVE IT. MY TOP TEN FAVOURITE THINGS ABOUT being fat. Ten-year-old me probably would have plugged her ears and yelled if I had tried to tell her any of this, or drowned me out with the *Shrek* soundtrack that she had at the ready in her Discman. But I wish she had known sooner that she didn't have to be built like Julia Stiles to be cool, hot and edgy. I wish she had known how safe and warm the body she hated so much was going to keep her over the years. I want fat people to revel in our fullness, in our boundlessness, in our freedom. While it's terrible to be squeezed out of all sorts of places and experiences, there is also a pretty radical party going on in the wide open spaces (yes, that's an intentional reference) that we create, painstakingly and out of necessity, for ourselves. I wish ten-year-old me had known that she was invited.

MY SUPERPOWER IS INVISIBILITY

Heather M. Jones

"I am big. I am fat. I am also good, and worthy,
and valued, and respected, and loved."

I WAS FIVE WHEN I LEARNED I WAS INVISIBLE. AS SUPERHUMAN abilities go, I would have preferred being able to fly. It would have been much easier to navigate and a whole lot cooler to my peers. I wasn't the only child to discover invisibility—Harry Potter had his Invisibility Cloak, after all—but unlike the boy wizard, to become invisible, all I had needed was my own body.

I was fat, and I quickly realized that meant I was not worth looking at. I didn't become invisible overnight. I did not wake up one day transparent but rather faded away slowly, like Marty McFly in the sibling photo he uses to gauge the success of his mission to the past. I didn't gain this superpower as a result of a lightning strike, toxic waste or the bite from a radioactive spider. It began with exclusion.

"You can't go on those monkey bars. You'll break them," said one of my pint-sized classmates. The small, wooden monkey bars in my kindergarten class were worshipped like an altar. They sat just outside the doorless washrooms, unused most of the time. The rule was, when Kermit the Frog was hanging from the frame, the monkey bars were closed—a clever tactic used by my seasoned kindergarten teacher to keep twenty five-year-olds from constantly asking to use them. Since they required an adult standing by to head off any broken limbs, the monkey bars were rarely open. Twenty years later, having become a kindergarten teacher myself, I would appreciate the self-preservation my teacher claimed in not opening this station regularly; but at five, we all believed this denial to be a form of torture.

Like everyone else, my eyes were constantly glued to Kermit throughout the day, waiting for him to vacate his perch on the bars. As soon as the amphibious crooner disappeared, I ran to join the others in line to swing my way across the four-foot horizontal ladder.

"You'll break them. You shouldn't be here," my classmate said to me. It was the first time I had really understood that the world viewed me as undeserving of occupying space. These monkey bars were for the kids in the class—but they weren't really for me. Each time I hung from the bars after this incident, I did so with trepidation instead of my previous reckless abandonment. I didn't swing wildly, feeling the wind in my skirt, but rather silently prayed the wooden rods would hold me, preventing the certain humiliation of falling, broken bar in hand, to the mats below. When I graduated from monkey bars, this fear would transfer to public chairs.

My body meant I was last to be picked for things, if I was picked at all. Captains were chosen, and the rest of us stood by waiting to hear our names called to be sorted into teams. That I would be last was never something I questioned—it was an inevitability. I was invisible; it made perfect sense that I would not be remembered until I became the last name on the list. I accepted this—I wouldn't want me on my team either.

I became fantastic at king's court, dodge ball's close cousin. I simply stood near the back and stayed quiet. No one threw the ball at me to get me out, and no one passed the ball to me to throw at others. It was only once the other team thought they had won, and I raised my hand when the teacher asked if anyone was still in the game, that I was noticed.

AS I GREW AND MY BODY DEVELOPED, IT WAS TIME TO LEARN THAT I couldn't rely entirely on my natural invisibility. Thankfully, I had lots of magazine articles to tell me how I could hide the parts of myself that were not fit for public view. I sought tips on which jeans to buy to minimize my thighs or to shave off my buxom hips. Which cuts of shirts would trim my waist and hide my shame? My teen magazines had all the answers, and I studied them as though there would be a quiz.

At thirteen, I decided I wanted to be an actor. It seemed a strange choice for someone who had spent her first decade on earth trying to blend in with the background; but upon closer examination, it made sense that I felt more comfortable and confident when I was being someone else. I didn't belong anywhere—but these characters were written right into the script. They had space created for them, and I was happy to ride their coattails.

I succumbed once again to the powers of advertising and signed up for classes at Barbizon School of Modeling and Acting. I was assured by the agent that the modelling part would be minimal, and I would shine in the acting portion. I believed them. I knew I could never be a model, but I was willing to endure a class or two of beauty tips in order to participate in what I was sure would be Actors Studio–level lessons in my chosen craft. I believed them—but they lied.

It was impossible to be invisible at Barbizon. The rooms had mirrors instead of walls—not mirrors on each wall but mirrors mounted like drywall, so that no matter where you looked, you saw your own reflection. Each lesson focused on a different aspect of our pubescent bodies and was taught by a picture-perfect, tall, slender model in the industry.

One Saturday morning, my teacher called us up in front of the class, one at a time, for us to guess what body type we each had. When it was my turn, I stood close to my statuesque instructor as she gathered my loose blouse in the back with one hand so that it would cling to my frame and give the other girls a better look at my body. "H," several of the girls called out with lackluster voices. H bodies were code for "wide all over." It was the one each of us dreaded being assigned, and I knew it was what I would be labelled by the would-be models in my class. I accepted my fate and was anxious to return to my spot on the carpet where I could look at my feet, avoiding my own gaze in the walls surrounding me.

"No, she has some curves," my teacher pointed out. It was true. At thirteen, I had the body of a twenty-year-old and was often mistaken for being older than I was because of my J-Lo hips and Bette Midler breasts. I was fat, but it wasn't distributed evenly; and while my waist was thick, I did have one, a fact confirmed in another class when every part of us was measured and our hip-to-waist ratios were calculated. I genuinely don't recall what I was eventually labelled, because it didn't matter. What mattered was that I was perceived as an H—simply big.

One week, we entered a room with a mirror on one wall only and a carpeted stage. I exhaled, thinking maybe this was the beginning of the acting sessions. Then I noticed the scale. As we had done with our body examinations, we were called one by one onto the stage to step on the scale. Our results were not private.

"One hundred fifty-three," said my teacher, as she recorded it in my handbook alongside the measurements of my chest, waist, hips and thighs. I could see the faces of the other girls watching in smug anticipation as I stepped onto the scale, and the looks of satisfaction in their correct guesses that I would be the heaviest in the class by a good margin.

I learned at Barbizon that it was not just my body that was big. On the Saturday that we traded the empty mirrored rooms for a mirrored room with chairs and lights, and a shelf to apply our makeup, my instructor held a magnifying glass an inch from my nose, her face so close to mine I could smell her gum, and informed me that I had large pores. I determined in this moment that being invisible, while demeaning, was preferable to being under a literal microscope.

The acting class did eventually come in the form of a simulated audition for a Keds sneaker commercial. For the first time in the roughly thirteen-week set of classes, I felt comfortable, and it showed. I sold the hell out of those shoes. I heard the usual whispering among the crowd—but this time the words were, "Wow, she's good."

I left modelling school determined to gain control over my power of invisibility. Could I make it come and go at will? I was comfortable being invisible, preferring to be ignored entirely than to have my shameful existence called attention to.

As it turns out, there was no in-between for me. Invisibility or blinding spotlight, those were my realities. I was accepted to an arts high school, throwing myself willingly into a literal spotlight. I felt comfortable on stage, with the lights shining directly into my eyes, obscuring everything else. Rehearsals and acting spaces became places I could easily hide, like a chameleon, slipping into character or blending into my atmosphere. Theatre kids focus on the theatre, and they paid little attention to me while we were preparing to perform. I didn't fit in, but I didn't stand out. Those were safe spaces. I didn't feel as though I belonged with this crowd, nor did I feel accepted by them—but I felt my presence was more tolerated there than in the world at large. I had auditioned for a place there. I had literally earned a spot in this program. While most of my peers still didn't accept me as socially worthy, they couldn't deny that I had a right to be there. I played king's court, standing perfectly still in a room filled with activity, taking it all in, being part of the game without ever actually touching the ball.

Outside of drama classes and extracurricular plays, I was keenly aware and apologetic of the space I occupied, both literally and fig-uratively. When we piled into cars, I did not feel I had the status needed to claim the front seat. Sitting in the back, I made the space cramped for the other occupants. I turned as sideways as I could manage, placing as much of my ample bottom onto the car door as I could without being obvious, compromising my own safety to add inches between me and my much tinier friends.

At parties, I sat on the floor. Two people could fit in the place I took up on the couch—it wasn't fair for me to use up space. I began writing notes to my friends instead of speaking to them directly if I had anything of importance to say. I was better able to express myself if I didn't have someone looking at me. I didn't try on clothing when I went to the mall with other people. I didn't fit the clothes offered in the places they shopped, and while I happily waited for them in fitting rooms and offered helpful opinions on their impromptu fashion shows, I didn't feel entitled to do the same in reverse at stores that catered to my size.

My hesitation to occupy physical space extended to metaphorical space. Like the monkey bars, I knew that just because something was technically offered to everyone didn't mean that it was meant to include me. I didn't go to prom. I skipped the band ski trip and the annual student trip to Quebec City. I pushed down my desperate desire to experience New York City for the first time and stayed home while the rest of my drama class explored the greatest city on earth. I didn't go because I knew no one would voluntarily choose to share a hotel room with me or allow me in their travel group, and I didn't want to be a burden. I knew that face well, that face of students reluctantly saying yes when I asked if I could join them. That face that said "Sure," but meant "I guess so. I'm too polite to say no." That face the captain who lost the coin toss makes when I'm the last one available to pick. I gave up New York to avoid that face.

Over time, I did manage to perfect my invisibility. By the time I became an adult, I had grown less worried about taking up space because I knew I could travel through anywhere unnoticed. There was a paradox in the way my size, something that should make me stand out, instead made me unseen. I knew by then that no men were checking me out while I shopped for shoes. No women were wondering where I got my clothes. I was background atmosphere, I was inconsequential, and I was okay with that.

THEN I GOT PREGNANT AND EVERYTHING CHANGED. FOR THE FIRST time, I wanted people to see me, to see this beautiful thing that was happening to me. I was still largely invisible, too big naturally for people to notice a growing bump—but this time, I called attention to my body. I wore clothes that accentuated my curves, and the bigger I got, the happier I was. When my son was born, I continued to avoid the shadows. Unlike me, my baby was stunning. Unlike me, he drew attention wherever we went. People stopped us in the streets to compliment my child's eyes and liken them to mine—the only feature of mine I have ever considered beautiful. My baby was not afraid to occupy space. My baby made his presence known and demanded to be acknowledged. When I was with my baby, I automatically belonged. I joined a Baby and Me class, unapologetic for my existence. I had a baby. I had an in.

At this class, unlike in other public spaces, everyone had her own baby and was not interested in mine. Instead, they were interested in me. They didn't care that I was fat; they cared that I was a bleary-eyed new parent like they were. As we grew into parenthood, our discussions moved past how many hours we had slept that night and when to start solid foods, into genuine, adult conversation. To the surprise of the thirteen-year-old inside of me, these women still didn't care that I was fat. They didn't care that I was occupying the space—they held a place open for me.

It's been eleven years since I joined that class, but I have never gone back to feeling as though my body were the determining factor in my value. This doesn't mean that I'm not still keenly aware of my size. I still pray for public chairs to hold me. I still avoid couches if only the middle section is left. I still, even at nearly forty years old, get called fat when someone disagrees with something I say and wants to hurt me. I still enjoy being invisible sometimes.

The difference now is that I am honest with myself about my body. I am big. I am fat. I am also good, and worthy, and valued, and respected, and loved, and none of those are mutually exclusive with the shape or size of my body. Being called fat used to be my biggest fear—I now see it as a neutral and accurate description of one facet of me. It doesn't hurt me, no matter the intentions of the person trying to weaponize it against me. I do not take up space; I demand it. I do not apologize for the space I occupy; I command it.

I've since spoken to many of those people who simply tolerated my presence in high school. It turns out I wasn't invisible to them. It seems my invisibility back then was less Harry Potter cloak and more "Emperor's New Clothes." They saw me. They liked me. They sought me out to reconnect as adults, and I now consider many of them among my inner circle of friends. I should have gone to New York.

I won't pretend that the insecurities never pop by uninvited or that I don't ever suddenly find myself feeling as though the room were covered in mirrors—but now, I don't look at my shoes. I look into the beautiful eyes I passed down to my children.

If they ever invent a time machine, I'm going to find that chubby little girl in kindergarten, afraid to break the solid wood. I'm going to tell her to rip that frog off those bars and climb her heart out. I'm going to tell her that if anyone ever tries to tell her she doesn't belong somewhere because of her body—swing harder.

THE FAT GIRL'S GUIDE TO EATING AND DRINKING

Christina Myers

"See how the fullness of your breasts is like the heavy weight of fruit that's ready to be picked, solid and lovely in the hand, delicious."

Tip 1: Salad, salad, salad

ALWAYS ORDER THE SALAD. IT'S THE LEAST LIKELY TO PROMPT DIR-ect questions like "I thought you were on a diet—can you have that?" or indirect and passive-aggressive observations like "Oh, gosh, I wish I could eat pasta, but I just feel so guilty about it after. Good for you for not worrying about such silly things," or worst of all, long meaningful glances at your plate and your mouth.

Salad is safe. Salad is virtuous. Just monitor the toppings and dressings; otherwise someone will point out they saw an article in a magazine last month about how salads nowadays are way, way, way worse than a cheeseburger and fries, all loaded up with ranch dressing and eggs and bacon bits and stuff. Then you've just wasted your order, opting for the virtue of a salad but still getting heat for a cheeseburger.

Go simple. House salad. No creamy dressings. Do they have a smaller version, a half order? Even if you know they don't, ask anyway. You're trying. Never forget this: if you can't be beautiful, at least try to be.

No one can say you're not trying.

Tip 2: Set the stage for validating your right to eat

NOTE HOW LITTLE YOU'VE EATEN, AS SOON AS POSSIBLE AFTER SIT-ting down, but only in a casual tone. "Oh my goodness, what a day! I've been so busy I haven't had a chance to stop since I got up this morning. I just worked right through lunch since I knew I was coming to meet you for dinner."

See? You deserve a decent dinner. You work hard. You've been going all day. You even gently implied that you possibly skipped breakfast, and you clearly noted the skipped lunch. Now pray that the co-workers you went for lunch with don't happen to pass by and stop to talk. It could happen. Having lunch *and* dinner would seem a tad extravagant, wouldn't it, for a girl like you? Don't open the door to criticism by suggesting you eat. Or that you enjoy eating. Now open your menu and order the salad (see Tip 1).

Tip 3: Monitor your consumption

EAT AS SLOWLY AS YOU POSSIBLY CAN. TALK A LOT, AS THOUGH YOU aren't starving from pretending food doesn't exist all day, as though eating is not your primary motivation to be here.

When your plate is half-empty, comment on how full you are, as though a regular serving of salad (see Tip 1) is just too much for you. They need to know: you're not just trying to be thinner; you clearly have the constitution of a thin person, don't you? It's like a quirk of nature, the Bermuda Triangle of Bodies, that somehow you don't even enjoy eating and you consume hardly anything and yet here you are, still plus-sized. Sympathy for your sad plight is only a fraction better than judgment, but it's better all the same.

Don't be the first one to finish (even if you ordered the smallest item). Leave something on your plate. Leave something carb-y on your plate. If you leave the cherry tomatoes but you eat the bread, no one will be fooled.

Tip 4: Enjoy the party, just not too much

AT A PARTY, CARRY A GLASS OF SODA WATER WITH LEMON AND stand at the opposite end of the room from the food. If you find your-self within a dozen feet of the buffet, everyone will assume you're hovering. They're watching, of course. All those foods are there for people who aren't fat; everyone knows queso and tortilla chips are a reward for being thin. You fat girls are welcome to approach the cru-dités platter, and you may swipe the tip of the raw asparagus into the bowl of herb-and-garlic veggie dip.

Don't double-dip: that's just a disservice to all the other large ladies out there who are trying so hard to ensure that people don't think we're all a bit messy and slovenly and crude. Dip once. Enjoy. Eat the rest of the asparagus plain. Go back for a carrot stick (just one—remember your roommate told you that carrots are super-duper high in sugar, so you may as well eat a doughnut as have a bowl of carrots). After the carrot, switch to celery. If absolutely necessary, have a few mushrooms. They're mostly water. Do you drink enough water? Looks like you might be retaining; drink more.

Tip 5: Consider your audience, always

WHEN YOU ASK FOR A MONTEREY JACK CHICKEN TAQUITO AT 7-Eleven, don't make eye contact with the guy behind the counter. Put your Perrier and sugar-free gum up on the counter first, like an apology. "See, Mr. Cashier, it's just Perrier. No calories. And the gum too. I'm trying, right?"

If you have been careful in selecting when to line up, there will be no high-risk individuals in line behind you to see what you're buying. It's unlikely anyone will say anything (though we all know they do from time to time, don't they?), but a long meaningful glance at your food purchase, or an eye roll and smirk, will definitely be unpleasant even without a verbal remark.

High-risk individuals include older men, younger men, thin men, fat men, men in suits, men in construction boots, very good-looking men, very unattractive men, teenaged boys and—more often than not—thin teenaged girls, thin middle-aged women and thin old women. Basically, try to make sure you line up in front of kids or other fat women. Or better yet, go at 2:00 a.m., when you won't bother anyone with your eating. Who needs to see you doing that, anyway?

Tip 6: "On the go" doesn't mean invisible

IF EATING IN YOUR CAR, ENSURE YOU DO ALL CHEWING AND SWAL-lowing while the car is in motion. Eating while stopped at a red light is an invitation for the person in the car next to you to shout "fat bitch" from his open window. Can you blame him? It's like walking down a dark alley in a short skirt after drinking: you're just getting what you asked for at that point. You'll already get "fat bitch" in response to almost every perceived vehicular wrongdoing, so why invite more trouble?

Related: make sure any and all food garbage is cleaned out of your car daily. From time to time, a co-worker will walk out of the building with you, or another mom will ask for a lift after morning drop-off, and what will you have to say for yourself when they spot that chocolate-covered-granola-bar wrapper on the passenger seat? After all, your friend posted an article on Facebook just last week about granola bars having more sugar and fat than a Dairy Queen Peanut Buster Parfait. It said people who eat them are fools duped by the marketing machine. You don't want people to think you're a fool, do you? Just throw out the garbage.

Tip 7: Reconsider your thighs

WHEN LYING IN BED ON A RANDOM SATURDAY MORNING (BEFORE you are awake enough to have felt your hunger and then berated yourself for being hungry at all), notice unexpectedly, as you roll onto your side and the light from the window glows warm over your skin, that the shape of your hip is like the curve of a long, golden sand dune. Run the palm of your hand over it from your waist to your thigh. It's so strong. And soft. The smoothest skin anywhere on your body.

Then catch your reflection randomly in the bathroom mirror, the window at Starbucks, the rear-view mirror of your car, and suddenly, without intention, notice how the roundness of your cheeks makes your face electric and excited when you smile. See how the fullness of your breasts is like the heavy weight of fruit that's ready to be picked, solid and lovely in the hand, delicious. Discover how the slope of your shoulder is dusty with freckles, like constellations. Notice that your legs, your strong legs (so strong from carrying you so well all these years), are neither girly nor mannish but, simply, yours.

Go to a restaurant with friends and order a salad. Because actually you happen to love the salad and it's what you wanted, not because you wanted to apologize for eating. Order the salad and eat the whole thing, because you were hungry enough; or eat half of it, because you weren't. Then realize you didn't tell anyone when you last ate, and you didn't spend half the meal talking so it would look like your food wasn't important. Your food *is* important. It fills your golden sand-dune hips and your electric, excited smile and your starry-constellation shoulders and your strong, strong legs.

Reconsider your thighs. Reconsider everything.

Tip 8: Feed yourself

BREATHE. CLOSE YOUR EYES. SINK INTO YOUR BODY, RATHER THAN letting it float away from you, detached like a balloon on a string, separate and foreign. Hear what it's saying to you. Feel what it needs. Trust yourself. Trust yourself again, for the first time in a long time. For the first time that you can remember, maybe.

Feed yourself like your hunger is not a sin, like your body is not a crime, like you do not need to explain. Feed yourself like a celebration: fill up on good food and the kindness and forgiveness it implies. Feed yourself like you have not spent a lifetime crafting rules to make yourself belong, to make your existence permissible, to make yourself beautiful even a little bit.

Discover, at last, that you already belong—to yourself. Discover, finally, that you did not need permission to exist—you exist regardless of approval. Discover, at the end (which is now the beginning) that you are already beautiful—not just a little bit but in ways that are magic and endless and cannot ever be measured.

Eat. When you need to. What you want to.

Drink. When you need to. What you want to.

Listen, trust, hear, feel.

Repeat.

TAMING THE WILD TUMMY

Andrea Hansell

"I was a professional woman and a mother, I told myself ... and my body successfully did all the things it was supposed to do."

TUMMIES RUN IN THE FAMILY ON MY MOTHER'S SIDE. NOT CUTE, slightly rounded tummies, but enormous, fleshy mounds reminiscent of the Venus of Willendorf. I imagine that in some eastern European village hundreds of years ago, my dumpling-shaped ancestors walked around feeling good about their bodies because everyone they saw had the same protruding bellies. Unfortunately, some relative of mine decided to move to the United States, where her descendants would be confronted with a culture that valued matzo-flat middles.

My grandmother told stories of binding her torso with rags during the Roaring Twenties so she could fit into skinny flapper dresses. She tried in vain to make her long pearl necklace hang free and not get looped around the mound of her tummy. In the fifties and sixties, my mother and aunts stuffed their overflowing bounty into panty girdles. These stiff, flesh-coloured garments, to which stockings were attached with round metal clips, compacted their torsos so tightly that, as my girl cousins and I observed in fits of giggles, they made the cracks between their buttocks disappear. Years of watching my mother hold her breath and grimace as she tugged her girdle on to go to dinner parties, along with the ubiquitous Playtex "My girdle is killing me" commercials on TV, convinced me that I never wanted to wear this particular torture device. I hoped that by the time I came of age, big bellies would be considered attractive. Or perhaps voluminous flannel nightgowns would become the new daytime fashion.

I grew from a round little girl who was gently steered away from two-piece bathing suits to a preteen who, along with my mother, was strategically positioned behind tall plants in family pictures to "hide our bellies." I would look at the slender image of Twiggy slinking across a billboard and yearn desperately to look like her, although I recall wondering where she stored her intestines.

In adulthood I found a man who loved my tummy, or at least loved me despite my tummy. I dieted my way into a slim-cut wedding dress and practised sucking in my gut for weeks before the ceremony. But as soon as I had a ring on my finger, I encountered a new problem. Everywhere I went, people, even people I didn't know—a person walking a dog past my house, a waitress in a restaurant—would look directly at my waistline and say, "When are you due?" Clearly these people had never read Dave Barry's advice that you should never ask a woman if she's pregnant unless you see a head crowning between her legs.

Eventually I really did get pregnant—twice, in fact—and for a total of eighteen months of my life I felt attractive without worrying about holding in my tummy or how the waistlines of clothes hit me. But—surprise!—after my children were born, my belly looked bigger than ever, only now it sagged and dimpled in ways it hadn't before. I tried self-acceptance. I was a professional woman and a mother, I told myself, not a fashion model or a Barbie doll, and my body successfully did all the things it was supposed to do. But by then the starved ideal of Twiggy had given way to an emphasis on "toned," and the models in magazines and actresses on TV all had taut tummies lightly rippled with muscle. It was hard to love my

Pillsbury Doughgirl body while being constantly bombarded with these images.

Then my husband was elected president of the Michigan Psychoanalytic Society. His election was to be announced at the organization's fancy annual dinner at a country club in the tony suburbs of Detroit. I had attended this dinner before. I remembered feeling drab and underdressed in a black skirt and tailored blazer, while the wives of psychoanalysts from Birmingham and Bloomfield Hills floated around in frothy dresses that sparkled under the chandeliers. As the new first lady of the Psychoanalytic Society, I felt obliged to purchase a dress that was fancier than my work clothes.

After much hunting, I found the dress. It was a shimmery black and gold silk brocade, with a matching jacket edged with delicate beading. The neckline flattered my face, and the colours brought out the gold tones in my hair. "I love it!" I said, pirouetting in front of the three-way mirror outside the dressing room.

The saleswoman frowned and looked down at my middle. I knew this look well; it was the look with which my female relatives scrutinized each other at family gatherings to see whose body had succumbed to what they called "the tendency." Following her gaze, I saw that while the soft folds of the jacket hid most of my upper belly, there was a slight basketball effect just below the jacket hem, which distorted the designs in the fabric of the dress.

"You need shapewear under that," she said.

"Shapewear?" I said. "Like ... a girdle?"

"Oh, no, like Spanx," she said. Seeing my puzzled look, she explained, "It's the newest thing. It slims and shapes like a girdle, but it's lightweight and comfortable. Oprah Winfrey is a huge fan. So is Gwyneth Paltrow."

I had a hard time imagining why Gwyneth would want to further compact her pencil body with shapewear, but I could relate to Oprah.

"Shall I bring you a few different types in your size?" the saleswoman offered. I nodded.

The name Spanx, with its suggestion of spanking and skanks, had me picturing lacy, naughty-looking lingerie. The packages the saleswoman brought to me were decorated with pictures of slinky models and labelled with wink-wink names like Slim Cognito and Trust Your Thinstincts. I selected the package labelled Hide and Sleek, thinking that my grandfather, who had peddled ladies' panties for pennies during the Great Depression, could have bought a month's worth of inventory for the price of this one undergarment. When I pulled the Spanx out of the box, I saw that it was no flirty little panty but a hefty black casing that would armour me from bust to knee. It felt rubbery and ungiving, like a Goodyear tire or, I hated to say it, like my mother's girdle. Anyone trying to spank a pert bottom clad in this contraption would surely break a finger or two.

I knew I should try it on. But by that point I felt self-conscious and exhausted, and I had a dawning awareness that I was the designated driver of my daughter's gymnastics carpool that day and had no business leisurely perusing shapewear in a fancy store. "I'll take the dress and the Spanx," I said, retrieving my credit card from the messy depths of my purse.

On the evening of the big dinner, my husband came back from picking up the babysitter to find me engaged in an epic battle to stuff my bulk into the Spanx. "Are you sure that thing is the right size?" he asked.

"Why, yes," I said, doing my best imitation of Scarlett O'Hara. "I just need someone to lace me into it."

Spurred to heroic action by the humiliation of being observed, I took a few deep breaths and tugged the Spanx into place. Still holding my breath, I slid the dress over my head and buttoned the jacket. And—oh, Spanx, my new fairy godmother!—I was utterly transformed. I looked around for my coachman and chariot, then settled for my husband and his Honda Accord.

No first lady of the Michigan Psychoanalytic Society ever made a grander entrance than I did that night. I glided into the elegant ballroom at the country club, where my dress was pronounced "stunning" by the analysts' wives, whose names I could never remember. As I sipped my gin and tonic during the cocktail hour, I kept looking down in awe at my smooth, flat midsection.

The problem started at dinner. My Spanx clearly did not want me to sit down in the straight-backed dining chair at my assigned table. It resisted folding, and paid me back for forcing it to change its natural stiff shape by gripping my torso so firmly and uncomfortably that it seemed to grow teeth and claws. No longer my fairy godmother, it became Maleficent, the Snow Queen, the Wicked Witch of the West. Above the top of it, just under my bosom, a screaming roll of flesh escaped its grasp and pushed up against my bra. A similar roll attempted a jailbreak at the bottom, just above my knee. The rest of me, alas, remained captive.

I bit into a warm, fragrant piece of sourdough bread, chewed, swallowed and felt the smooth, starchy ball lurch to a stop in the portion of my esophagus just above my Spanx. I burped loudly.

"Are you okay?" the woman next to me asked.

"Yes," I mumbled. "Just, um, not that hungry."

I pushed my food around on my plate and decided to go with liquids only. That was a mistake. The wine went straight to my head and the water went straight to my bladder, which had shrunk to a tenth of its normal size under the pressure of the Spanx. I was about to excuse myself to go to the ladies' room when my husband was called to the podium. I sat through the ensuing long speeches trying desperately not to pass out or wet my Spanx. When my husband thanked his lovely wife and all eyes turned momentarily toward me, I gamely flashed a smile that felt like a grimace. The minute the applause died down and people pushed their chairs back from the tables, I hobbled off to the ladies' room.

The Spanx was almost as hard to get off as it was to put on. Once it was safely down around my ankles, I knew there was no question of wedging myself back into it. I had deep red welts in my flesh where it had bitten into me. My liberated belly was channelling Lynyrd Skynyrd and singing out that it was free as a bird now, and this bird you cannot change.

I slid the Spanx off over my shoes, wadded it into a stiff ball and tried to stuff it into my little black dress purse. This worked as well as trying to feed an elephant to a mouse. I decided impetuously that since I'd never wear it again, I might as well throw it away, fifty-dollar price tag be damned. As I was about to take aim for the discreet little hole in the marble countertop through which classy country club ladies tossed their used paper towels, the ladies' room door opened.

"Congratulations!" I heard from a velvety throat as high heels clicked their way across the floor to me.

I quickly shoved the wad of Spanx inside my jacket and under my arm—my right one, since my purse was over my left shoulder.

"Thank you, Carol," I said. (Was it Carol? Or Kathy? I hoped it was Carol.) Then, murmuring that I had to go find my husband, I dashed out the door, Spanx ball firmly clasped between my arm and my side.

My husband was standing in the long line for the valet parking. As we stood there, one couple after another came up to congratulate us and shake our hands. With my right elbow pinned to my side to keep the Spanx secured in my armpit, I could give only little flipper handshakes. I thought I must look like my neighbour's corgi when it was given the command "Paw" and stuck its short leg out from its barrel of a body. But an odd handshake was far preferable to having my Spanx tumble out and land on someone's shoe.

The car was brought, the valet tipped, and I finally shifted the Spanx to my lap. Still feeling the effects of drinking on an empty stomach, as well as my liberation from sadistic undergarments, I was cheerful and chatty on the way home. When my husband offered me an after-dinner mint he had taken from the valet stand, I said, "No, spanx," and laughed heartily at my own joke, my newly freed belly shaking with mirth.

"What's up with you?" my husband said. "You usually hate these dinners."

"I guess I overdid the wine," I said, and, to be generous, added, "And I'm happy that you're happy. Congratulations, Mr. President."

An hour later, while my husband drove the babysitter home, I sat in the kitchen smearing apple slices with peanut butter to make up for my skipped dinner. It occurred to me that I no longer had the Spanx. What had I done with it after transferring it to my lap in the car? Had it turned into a pumpkin at midnight?

The front door opened and my husband walked into the kitchen. He was gingerly holding my black Spanx like it was some kind of injured animal.

"Lose something?" he said.

"Where was it?" I asked.

"Heather found it in the yard on the way out to the car."

"Oh, God," I said. "What did she say?"

"She said, 'Excuse me, Mr. Hansell, but I found this in your flower bed.'"

"And you said?"

"I said, 'Oh, that's Mrs. Hansell's underwear. She was wearing that earlier tonight.' Heather seemed really embarrassed. Should I not have said 'underwear' in front of a fourteen-year-old?"

I gave him a look.

"What?" he said.

"Do you think maybe she was embarrassed because she thought you removed my underwear in our front yard?"

"Oh," he said. "I didn't think of that."

He tossed the Spanx onto the table next to the peanut butter jar and put his arms around me.

"Why did you wear that thing, anyway?" he said. "You look fine without it. Care to join me in the flower bed?"

"Yes, spanx," I said.

FACADES OF FAT

Elizabeth Cook

"No one told me I had a problem. The only thing people saw was a girl achieving the most important thing in the world: losing weight."

FAT AS FAILURE: 204. THE NUMBERS SHE SAID OUT LOUD OOZED with repulsion. It was grade eight, and it was mandatory that each student be weighed for a public health census. This was my first memory of being judged by a number on a scale, not by my intelligence, athleticism or creativity. By a number. The "normal" girls in the class chittered about the numbers they received as though they were test scores, comparing them to see who came out ahead, something to be proud of. With that, I knew I had failed, for the first time in my life.

FAT AS SHAME: MY MOTHER PARKED THE CAR AT THE BACK OF THE hospital by the dumpsters, near the back door that led to the morgue and industrial supply rooms, the bowels of the hospital that were never to be acknowledged. It was our first visit to the dietitian.

FAT AS LAZY: I SAT ON THE DOCTOR'S EXAMINATION TABLE WHILE he and my mother discussed me as though I weren't even there, trying to determine what was wrong with me. The term *fat* was thrown around like a symptom of a disease; *obese* would have been too delicate a word for the impression the doctor was trying to impart on us. He said matter-of-factly (when in essence he knew nothing of my existence outside of my chart) that I was a couch potato. I was seven years old, and I knew then what it was to feel judged by an adult.

FAT AS UNLOVABLE: I HAD MY FIRST PUPPY LOVE FROM AGE EIGHT to eleven. Michael. He was my best friend, a neighbour and a member of our usual gang. We had professed our love for each other at a simple age when silly things like body image weren't even on our radar yet, but by the time we reached eleven years old, puberty had begun and there it was—dirty old body image. One night he called and I could hear the voices of his friends in the room with him; he had left a note earlier in the day saying he needed to speak to me that night. The purpose was to break it off with me: "Why would I want to go out with a fat cow like you?" And then, from the friends around him, laughter. After that, the only time I received attention from boys was when I had lost weight. In my mind it was because I was smaller. Never mind that I was happier, more confident and outgoing; it had to be because of the number on the scale.

FAT AS STUPID: I EXCELLED IN SCHOOL; IT WAS EASY FOR ME. BUT even though I consistently achieved top grades, I was always overlooked for enrichment classes. These classes were for students that didn't require extra time for reading and writing. It wasn't until a teacher in grade six, Mrs. Janes, asked why. Why wasn't I in enrichment? I knew why: I was never even considered because I was fat and therefore, by default, stupid.

FAT AS OBSESSION: IN MY EARLY TWENTIES I MANAGED TO LOSE A lot of weight and almost reached the goal weight that I'd had in my head since that fateful day in grade eight—135 pounds. The lowest I reached was 141 and I thought I was dying. Weight loss had become an addiction, but an acceptable addiction. It was the only thing that mattered. I would weigh myself first thing every morning and then after every meal. I knew then I was putting that number on the scale before my own health; eventually I gave up. Losing the weight hadn't fixed my life as I thought it would: I was still in my crappy job, I still had no money, and I never did feel thin. I knew that particular weight was unmanageable, I knew I was sick, and I didn't know how to fix it, so I went back to what was easy for me. Back to being fat, because that had actually never changed.

No one told me I had a problem. The only thing people saw was a girl achieving the most important thing in the world: losing weight. My cousin told me I looked great, and I responded with "Thanks, but I weigh myself five times a day."

"Whatever it takes," she said.

I know she had her own body issues to deal with. Even though she was a healthy runner, she spent her life running away from a prevalent obesity gene that scourged her family. My friends who had seen me through various sizes were concerned for me because I was so thin, but they never said anything. Until after.

FAT AS FEAR: I SEE MOTHERS OUT WITH THEIR CHUBBY LITTLE girls and I think, *Thank God that's not me*. I feel that disgust, shame and blame that I would never want any child to feel—the way that I felt. If I were a mom to girls, would I make them feel that way? The idea terrifies me. I have two boys and they will never know what it's like to grow up as a fat girl. It's your entire definition, and that's all you will be known as—the BIG one. Not the smart one, or the funny one, or the active one. Fat trumps all else. Even now my oldest boy, at eight, knows the word *fat*—he calls it the F-word. He knows because his friends made fun of his fat mom. He knows embarrassment because of fat, because of me. It surprised me that, no matter how progressive and accepting we become in our society, welcoming all walks of life and backgrounds, something as insignificant as your body shape will determine how other people see you and treat you. Fat seems to be the last acceptable discrimination, and it's everywhere.

FAT AS EVOLUTION: FROM WHEN I WAS A YOUNG CHILD TO A TEEN-ager to where I am today—a forty-year-old wife, mother and full-time employee—these themes continue to reintroduce themselves into my life. But they bring new meaning and awareness to the person I am evolving into, and about the person I was back then. My personal concept of success in my life is incongruent with how I perceive my body: still feeling fat as failure, or shame, or fear, or stupidity. It's ridiculous, I know. To be successful in whatever area you pursue isn't negated if you happen to look a certain way. But these inaccurate beliefs have had such a stronghold on my life that I have to wonder if I don't end up self-sabotaging myself as a way of fulfilling that prophesy.

Have I stopped myself in the past from participating in life because of how I feel I look? You betcha! Have I backed away from opportunities because of the intense anxiety that I would be seen by strangers? Of course I have.

But no longer.

To the little girl who was always the biggest: You are beautiful. You are kind and funny and smart, and you have an intense imagination. Nothing can hold you back; don't let it. To the grown-up little girl who feels like the biggest: You are beautiful. Your body has achieved amazing feats and created amazing human beings. You are kind and funny and smart, and you have an intense imagination. Nothing will hold you back any longer.

MY BODY'S CIVIL WAR

Tara Mandarano

"I felt more accepted, more approved of, the less of me there was."

"WHY AREN'T YOU WEARING ANY PANTS?"

The question from my five-year-old daughter catches me off guard. I look down at myself in confusion, taking in my beloved black leggings. Her outraged tone implies I'm running around in my underwear, but in reality, I'm just wearing something elasticized that feels comfortable against my swollen belly.

"What do you mean?" I ask her, seeking clarification, but half-afraid of what might come out of her unfiltered mouth.

"They look like tights."

Ah. There it is. One of my biggest insecurities innocently vocalized by this pint-sized version of me. The worry that I am constantly being judged and scrutinized for the way I look.

I REMEMBER MY MOTHER ALWAYS TELLING ME WHAT A GOOD appetite I had, even as a child. As family lore goes, sometimes she would even save me the biggest pork chop when we had our extended family over for dinner, much to the consternation of my dad and uncle. Back then I could basically eat whatever I wanted with no worries about my weight. Up until that point, I always had seconds as a matter of course. I enjoyed ice cream and endless hamburgers. Bread. Pop. Cheese. Potatoes. As an adolescent, I was a lean, mean metabolizing machine.

Then one summer I suddenly developed seasonal allergies and couldn't fit into my shorts anymore. I remember being puzzled that I had to go up two sizes out of the blue. I had been used to being a "perfect" size 6 for quite some time, just like the Wakefield twins in the Sweet Valley High series I devoured as a teen. Buying size 10 clothes made me feel like a frumpy failure. I couldn't figure out what I had done wrong to end up in double digits.

It wasn't until I was in my mid-twenties that I was diagnosed with PCOS (polycystic ovary syndrome). I was living in Dublin, Ireland, at the time, and one day I experienced excruciating pelvic pain while taking a shower. I immediately knew something serious was going on, and an ultrasound at the hospital revealed one of many ovarian cysts I would be cursed with over the years. PCOS was actually an incidental finding. It meant that my hormones were wildly out of whack and that my ovaries were covered in tons of small, fluid-filled follicles containing immature eggs that would not grow enough to trigger ovulation.

At hearing this news, a lot of mysterious things began to make sense. PCOS also meant I had higher-than-normal male hormones (androgens) coursing through my body. Now I understood why I had suffered from oily skin and persistent acne since the age of eleven. Now I knew why I had hair growing in places that usually only old ladies complained about. Being in my twenties, the aesthetic effects of PCOS were my primary concern. Since I was slim again, back into single-digit clothing sizes, probably between a size 6 and a size 8, and definitely in the "lean" category of the disorder, eliminating spots and unwanted facial hair were my top priorities.

I also did a glucose tolerance test after my diagnosis, since PCOS can also contribute to more serious long-term health conditions like diabetes and heart disease, but it was normal. So off I went, with my birth control pills in one hand and my spironolactone (an anti-androgen medication) in the other, thinking my body and weight could be forever kept in line by medications.

That would turn out to be wishful thinking.

MY WEIGHT WOULD ALWAYS FLUCTUATE OVER THE NEXT TEN years, but it didn't seem to be down to anything I did or didn't do. I ate the same. I didn't exercise much. I didn't change my pills. The only new thing in my life was the insidious presence of endometriosis. It had actually first invaded my body in that ominous cyst I felt twisting in the shower. The doctor had called it a classic "chocolate cyst," or an endometrioma, because it was filled with old blood.

But I underestimated the invisible effect of endo on my life. Whenever it flared up and tissue from my uterus grew in places it shouldn't, I put on weight. It was as if my whole body was inflamed, and it was. Struggling to fit into my usual clothes was always a sign that something wasn't right internally. I remember feeling so defeated going through those vicious hormonal cycles, having to buy bigger clothes to fit my ever-expanding tummy.

At one point the pain got so bad that my gynecologist decided to put me into fake menopause to shut down my reproductive system and give it a break before my next surgery. I received two injections of Decapeptyl in the mid-2000s, and my period went AWOL for six months. I loved not being in discomfort every month, but I hated the fact that I ballooned into the "big" version of me again. Suddenly I was solid. Plump. My face looked like a chipmunk's. I also had to deal with hot flashes and night sweats, but feeling fat was my main complaint.

Six months later, I had my surgery and my doctor proclaimed it a success. Within weeks, the pounds started falling off of their own accord, since the meds had worn off. Snug pants were suddenly hanging from my waist. My face started to look more like itself. I basked in the glow when co-workers and friends exclaimed, "You look so good!" because I knew that was code for "Congratulations! You look so much better now that you've lost a few pounds! Now tell us how you managed to do it so quickly! What are your secrets?"

I HAD MOVED HOME TO CANADA AFTER SEVEN WONDERFUL YEARS in Dublin and had met my soulmate while working at a romance novel company. A couple of years into our relationship, we started trying for a baby. I was thirty-five, and it was a high priority for me. Because of my background with PCOS and endometriosis, I wasn't even convinced I could have kids.

When nothing happened after a few months, I was referred to a fertility specialist. She immediately put me on metformin, a diabetic drug that also helps women with PCOS lose weight and ovulate. I took it without question, even though I wasn't really carrying around any extra pounds. I also decided to see a naturopath during this time, to even Western and Eastern medicine out, and I promptly started six weeks of acupuncture, along with various supplements and Chinese herbs.

Between going off the pill, starting metformin and committing to this holistic protocol, I unexpectedly lost ten pounds in about a month. It was the thinnest I'd been in a long time, and I was thrilled. My collarbone was so prominent. It didn't look as if I had an ounce of fat. Once again, everybody in my social circle noticed and commented on my new body, but they never came right out and said anything explicit about my weight.

Psychologically, it felt like I was being covered in a warm fuzzy blanket of compliments. People told me how nice I looked in outfits that had never elicited any form of praise before. I didn't care. I felt more accepted, more approved of, the less of me there was.

I REMEMBER BEING SO PROUD OF MYSELF FOR GAINING ONLY thirty-five pounds when I was pregnant. I had heard stories of women putting on fifty, sixty, seventy pounds. I thought it was all about self-control. Willpower. Not overdoing it on the doughnuts. Now I know it's way more complex than that. While everyone I knew was complimenting me in my early pregnancy, saying how amazing I looked and that they couldn't even see a bump, I was actually unknowingly doing serious damage to my body.

I had read somewhere that continuing metformin while pregnant was beneficial for women with PCOS and that it helped prevent miscarriage. After having serious doubts I would ever get with child, there was no way I was going to mess about with stopping it and risk losing the baby. But I noticed that I wasn't feeling too great. Beyond the usual pregnancy symptoms, I would often get weak spells in which I felt faint or like I might pass out, and I desperately craved anything sugary. I remember calling my husband to meet me right off the subway one night after work.

"Bring lots of cookies," I told him, in a panic.

The next week, my endocrinologist called me herself to say that my blood sugar level was dangerously low, hovering around 2.5. She told me to stop the metformin immediately, cold turkey. I cried and asked her if I had somehow harmed the baby, but she answered that she was more worried about me.

"The baby will take what it needs," she brusquely advised me.

I didn't see any evidence of my baby's growth until I was well past five months along. It had become an obsessive worry to me, this lack of a noticeable bump, and I found it ironic that now I was concerned about not putting on enough weight. Each time I went to my OB appointment, the receptionist would take my blood pressure and ask me to stand on the scale—in the public waiting room. I dreaded that part of the process every time I went, especially toward the end of my pregnancy, when I reached my all-time high of 163 pounds.

Just don't let me gain more than 35, I would repeat to myself in my head, like a mantra. I also felt embarrassed for every other woman who had to announce her size to a room full of strangers. It just didn't feel right. It was needless exposure and forced vulnerability at a time when most mothers-to-be were already feeling anxious about everything going on with their bodies. But I never complained or stood up and said anything. I thought I was being extra sensitive, and I didn't want to offend anybody.

A MONTH AFTER MY DAUGHTER WAS BORN, I LOST MYSELF IN THE throes of postpartum depression and anxiety. I felt shell-shocked and overwhelmed in my new reality. I wasn't sleeping, I was in pain, and I absolutely hated breastfeeding. I had low milk supply, and I was barely coping—or peeing.

Something strange was also happening with my body. The weight was miraculously melting off. Somehow, I lost those thirty-five pregnancy pounds in a mere month. I wasn't trying, but I was rewarded with positive reinforcement at every turn anyway, as if I had achieved a massive accomplishment. I even remember my sister pulling up my sweater in the dead of winter to look at my suddenly flat belly. She was unbelieving.

Everyone kept saying how good I looked "after just having a baby." It didn't mean much to me at the time, because I was navigating such a maze of emotional misery. But of course, there was a small, dark part of me that cheered even as I physically disappeared. Why did other women always say it took up to a year to "get their body back"? Clearly, it didn't.

Now I know different. I have no idea why I lost the weight so quickly, but it was probably because I wasn't taking care of myself properly. I was barely eating. My main priority was trying to feed my daughter, even though my breasts weren't co-operating. I wasn't peeing because I was severely dehydrated and not drinking enough water.

But at least my pre-pregnancy jeans fit again.

IS THERE A STRICT GUIDE TO WHAT SOCIETY CONSIDERS PLUS-SIZED?

It's five years later, and I'm a size 12 at the moment, so I'm not quite sure where that puts me exactly. I can still shop in "regular-sized" stores, but I often find it's just all the smaller sizes they have left in stock. All of the size 12s and 14s have long been snapped up.

Psychologically, I feel like I'm living in a limbo land between what society considers "ideal" and being a true plus-sized person. One thing I know for sure, though: I am not happy with my body. I don't like being "curvy." I loathe the words *muffin top* and *chunky*.

I can't honestly embrace all my extra lumps when I see photographs or videos of myself, because it seems as if I am looking at a stranger. In my mind, I'm still the slim version of myself, and it's shocking to not see that reflected in photos. It makes me grieve for the girl I once was, even if it feels superficial.

Today I weigh 170 pounds. Today I weigh more than I did when I was pregnant. The shame associated with this fact is sometimes too heavy for my heart to carry. I feel like a loser. Like I have let myself go. And yet intellectually I know that it is not all my fault.

Part of me having "more than an inch to pinch" is that I've also been diagnosed with reactive hypoglycemia, insulin resistance and prediabetes in the last two years. This means my pancreas isn't working properly. I have too much insulin circulating in my body, and my cells aren't responding to it appropriately. Carbs aren't necessarily my enemy, but I have to limit them and pair them with protein to avoid graduating to full-blown type 2 diabetes. I have left the "lean" PCOS category and moved into the group that puts on weight easily because of underlying hormone issues in my body.

My endocrinologist has been extraordinarily patient with me. "Don't be so hard on yourself," she tells me kindly.

She says avoiding low blood sugar episodes that can be life threatening is far more important than losing weight. She says to keep taking my antidepressant for my mental health, even though it's not helping my insulin levels. She says that being able to function and be a mother and a wife has to be my priority.

I nod and try to keep the tears in my eyes and off my cheeks, but once outside her office, I always feel like crying. It's been three months since I saw her last, and I haven't lost any damned weight. Again.

AS A WOMAN, I CONSTANTLY NAVIGATE A SIZE-OBSESSED WORLD. Sometimes I refuse to buy a "large" piece of clothing on principle, even if it's a better fit. For me, it's like admitting defeat. From my own personal experience, there's no better compliment than to hear that I've lost weight, even if it isn't true. During particularly low times, I long to hear those magical, elusive words, even though I know I shouldn't place my self-love and self-acceptance so much in the hands of others.

I don't like mainly wearing elasticized pants. I don't like fearing jeans. I don't like changing in another room so my husband won't see me naked. I hate feeling that I need to hide as much of myself as possible, wrapped up in black clothes, concealed under floating tops or long cardigans. But that's my life.

These days I swing between trying to be more body positive and still loathing the way I look. I post a lot of selfies to social media (mainly of my face) because I'm seeking approval that people still find me attractive, even if my appearance has transformed so much.

I constantly struggle with body-image issues, even when I consciously try to stop my negative self-talk and just get on with things. My closet feels like a torture chamber, sorely limited in what I can actually wear, full of oversized tops and leisure-wear pants. The pretty dresses and more form-fitting tops taunt me. Sometimes when I'm alone and there's no chance of being seen, I'll try something on from my "old" life, before I gained thirty pounds and lost most of my self-confidence. Inevitably it will feel tight or get stuck somewhere around my thighs, and I will sigh and fling the offending top or pair of pants on the floor, disappointed and dejected that my preferred clothes don't fit me anymore.

It's difficult to dress your body when you suffer from a chronic illness that causes bloating. I'm always careful not to draw attention to my tummy, or "endo belly." If I'm honest, I really just want to hide my body. There are some days when I just want to be invisible so I don't have to encounter myself in the mirror. But I know that's not psychologically healthy.

And so I am determined to begin a journey to accept my body more. I'm just emotionally tired of constantly fighting and losing a civil war. And what for? My body may not be what it once was or at its prime, but I am still here on this earth, breathing and living and writing. Despite all my raging, my body is still keeping me alive. I try to remember this when I'm in pain or frustrated with how things don't fit.

So maybe I'll never be a Wakefield twin again. Perhaps it's my lot to look more like Bridget Jones. But who really cared about her weight or dress size after seeing that movie? It was her personality, sensitivity and hilarious vulnerability that attracted people. I want to accept myself just as I am while still working on making better choices when it comes to exercise and what I eat. And I don't think those two things are mutually exclusive.

Now, instead of rating a three out of ten on a scale of how much I love my body, I just focus on what parts are working right. A number doesn't have to define me. Being congratulated on being pregnant when I wasn't can just be a bad memory.

Instead, I try to focus on what makes me feel valued and worthy. I love my hair, my eyes and my freckles, and the fact that they cover nearly all of me. I'm also proud of my mind and my creativity. Over the last forty-one years, my body has been through thick and thin with me, and I'm making a real effort not to criticize it so much, both mentally and verbally.

After all, I have my five-year-old daughter standing by, constantly watching me. And I want her to accept herself in her entirety and not feel that she just has to be pretty. It's something I'm still figuring out and learning how to do, but it's all part of my healing.

EAT MY WORDS

Susan Alexander

---

*"I sometimes feel I have missed the best part of
my life struggling in my dark woods."*

I CONFESS THAT I BINGE.

Picture this: I escape from the demands of summer house guests, work and family for a few hours of writing. But it is as if the house were enchanted and every doorway led to the kitchen. I find myself inexplicably in front of the open fridge door. I rummage in the jammed freezer, dig out a massive brownie, slather on ice cream and wolf it down. It does not taste half as good as I had imagined. (Had I really been imagining this?) Out comes the chocolate sauce. That is better. In fact it is so good that I get a bowl of ice cream and pour on more sauce. That is even better than the brownie.

"What else?" I murmur, opening the cupboard. I find toasted hazelnuts left over from yesterday's salad. Chocolate hazelnut is one of my top tastes in the world, and this discovery calls for another sundae: vanilla ice cream, the last of the chocolate sauce and toasted hazelnuts. This is approaching the fantasy flavour that I seek. I am as close to satisfied as it is possible to get during a binge. True satisfaction is always elusive. "The road of excess leads to the palace of wisdom," William Blake wrote in *Proverbs of Hell*. It would have been helpful if he had noted that the road might kill you long before you reach the palace.

So what led to the binge?

It was because I had to be nice to a British colleague turned house guest who was visiting for a few days and allergic to our two cats.

It was because the house guest's seven-year-old son had wandered into a wasp nest five minutes after their arrival.

It was because my daughter was just two days home from a year away in Australia and I was ignoring her to entertain house guests.

It was because I sent her to the store with a list and she had not bought the key ingredient for making pie pastry. She thought Tenderflake was a breakfast cereal. She was innocent of the existence of lard.

It was because I was stressed about that night's dinner party.

It was because I wanted to write and could not find words.

It was because I despised myself for not being able to cope with guests and children and writing and dinner parties and turning fifty; because I wondered whether my marriage was really working, whether I was helping out enough with my aging mother, whether my two nieces were going to die from cancer; because my youngest would be leaving home next year and I could not remember who I was outside of being Mum.

It was because I was not sure how to make pastry, and what was I, a certifiable sugar junkie, doing making pie for tonight's dinner party anyway, to say nothing of having a fridge stocked with ice cream, brownies and chocolate sauce?

For most of my life, eating was the solution to all my problems.

Today it does not work.

It never has.

I have been doing this as long as I can remember.

I am reminded of Albert Einstein's definition of insanity: doing the same thing over and over again and expecting different results.

As if one confession were not enough, now I must admit that later the same night, after the kitchen was clean and everything put away,

I found myself back in front of the fridge with a fork, listening to the whispers of my leftover pies. Blackberry and apple. My daughter and a friend were playing cards in the next room. Everyone else had left or gone to bed. There was no question of hunger after a substantial dinner, pie, wine, chocolates, a cheese plate and fruit. But I wanted more.

For me, despair tastes like the pie in the laundry room. That is where I hid and ate. I worried about getting caught but I could not stop. I had the feeling that I never would get enough.

Why are eight slices of pie in an evening not enough? Why is half a box of chocolates not enough? How many brownie and chocolate hazelnut sundaes are enough? Why is a full day of binging, on top of three square meals, in which I consumed enough calories to fuel a person for five days, not ENOUGH?

The short answer is that no amount of food can ever be enough because I am not hungry. "If it's not hunger, then food won't fix it": so says one of my favourite truisms. If it is not hunger I am feeling, then what is it?

I used to break up my intense binging from time to time with other kinds of disordered eating: a month of fasting, a year of purging. For decades, I dieted and I binged. I exercised and I binged. I got married and I binged. I read about how to lose and keep off weight and I binged. I journalled about why I binged, and how I felt before, during and after, and I binged. I found God and I binged. I raised my children and I binged. I lived a full, productive, exciting, adventurous life and still I binged.

Every emotion feels like hunger to me. Anger. Anxiety. Loneliness. Sadness. Fatigue. Fear. Even the good ones, happiness, passion, love, feel like hunger. Binging saw me through childhood trauma, teenage angst, university stress, travelling, professional life, marriage and motherhood.

I always imagined that if I tried hard enough, had a plan and stuck to it, had enough willpower and commitment, I could control myself. Even after decades of successive failures, I refused to face the fact that my eating, and, in a sense, my life, was out of my control and I was powerless to do anything about it.

Every change involves a moment of reckoning followed by a process. My moment arrived when I was alone. I had been trying to control my eating but constantly failing and falling into binging. Even my "fat clothes" were getting tight. I was alone with an unsafe person. Myself.

Evening approached. I wandered with my dog down a path into darkening woods. Then I caught sight of far-off brilliance. Red, orange and magenta gleamed through the thick, dark trees. The whole sky was aflame. I was missing it. As I raced back, I could see it draining to grey. Short of breath and sweating, I ran past the beach and scrabbled up a rocky outcropping with a west view. The glorious brightness had faded, but from here I could see a lingering glow over a nearby island. The surrounding sky, gold and pale blue, was reflected in the silvered surface of the sea. The backdrop of mountain was deep purple. A windswept cloud hung above the scene.

I sometimes feel I have missed the best part of my life struggling in my dark woods. Yet that evening the sunset was still beautiful and only fading slowly. I sat and watched it for a long time, and the red glow stayed. Maybe I would get enormous, maybe I would get healthy. I did not know why I had this problem, but I finally accepted it. I became thankful for the beauty of the evening, thankful for my life.

Remember learning to float? How the body must relax first to find, and then trust, its hidden buoyancy in water. We discover that water can hold us while we learn how to move in it. Everything else is just technique and practice. Moments of freedom from food obsession are like floating.

Shortly after that sunset, I had my first experience of having a strong desire to binge and suddenly having a choice not to act. I do not remember what triggered the desire to eat compulsively. It could have been an escalation of Hurricane Menopause raging relentlessly over the Gulf of Midlife. It might have been another argument with my husband that left me feeling lonely. Perhaps it was the chest-constricting pressure of meeting a deadline. Or maybe it was a call from a sobbing child who needed advice and comfort. All of these turn up the heat of emotions, which cool in the promising white light of the fridge interior.

The "why" of a binge is unimportant. What I remember is not doing what I always had done. Something inside me was inexplicably changed. I pushed the fridge door shut and dragged my feet out of the kitchen. Sadness then washed over me like a rogue wave out of a calm sea. I lost my footing and went under. I could not breathe in the roiling boil of my feelings, but I did not fight the downward drag. I sank into my deep-sea sadness and eventually I emerged, still alive. I had survived without reaching for the old, sodden life jacket of excess food.

Binging has been my PFD, but it lost its buoyancy.

I am learning to float.

Photo by TwinLens Photography

EDITOR

CHRISTINA MYERS IS AN AWARD-WINNING NEWSPAPER JOURNAL-
ist turned freelance writer and editor. After leaving her long-time
newsroom post, she turned her attention to more creative work,
including both fiction and narrative non-fiction (and sometimes,
secretly, poetry, too.) She holds degrees in journalism and psychology from Thompson Rivers University and the University of British
Columbia, respectively, and is an alumna of the Writer's Studio at
Simon Fraser University. A fan of vintage collectibles and big dresses
with deep pockets, she juggles parenthood and creative work from
her home outside Vancouver, BC.

CONTRIBUTORS

Susan Alexander has been called "a big girl" since the day she was born. She is the author of *The Dance Floor Tilts*, a book of poems. Her work has appeared in chapbooks and several literary magazines. One poem is currently riding the Vancouver buses (Poetry in Transit, 2018–19). Susan lives on Bowen Island, BC, which she acknowledges as the traditional, unceded territory of the Squamish Nation.

Emily Allan is a freelance writer, editor and equality consultant whose work deals with intersectional feminism and body politics. Born and raised on a little island in British Columbia, she relocated in 2018 from Vancouver to Toronto, where she now runs a small writing group, affectionately and accurately named Snack Club. She holds a BA in anthropology and political science and an MA in anthropology from the University of British Columbia.

Jen Arbo lives with her family in New Westminster, BC, where she works in the public sector. She holds a blue belt in karate, prefers to shoot her recurve bow sightless and cans a great jar of jam, though she swears she is not preparing for a dystopian future. Likes: snug socks, strong tea and a brand new dot-grid journal. Dislikes: heights, clutter and storage containers that have lost their matching lids. "Encircled" is her first published piece since her son was born and stole her brain a decade ago, and she's happy to be back. You can find her online on various platforms as @jenarbo.

Shadoe Ball is a writer and artist from Sudbury, Ontario, who lives in Toronto. She was diagnosed with binge eating disorder at twenty-eight years old. Through group therapy programs, a HAES-informed nutritionist and a lot of self-discovery, she learned healthier coping mechanisms for stress and anxiety, such as flexing her creative muscles. She is thrilled to be included in this anthology and is eager for opportunities to connect with big ideas and curious people.

Dr. Rohini Bannerjee, born and raised in Dartmouth, Nova Scotia, daughter of immigrants from Himachal Pradesh, India, is an associate professor of French and francophone studies in the Department of Modern Languages and Classics and a faculty member in the Asian studies, women and gender studies and international development studies programs at Saint Mary's University in Halifax. Her primary research focuses on the literatures and cultures of the francophone Indian Ocean. Her poetry has appeared in *Understorey Magazine* and a short story in *India in Canada, Canada in India* (Cambridge Scholars, 2013). When she is not teaching or writing, Rohini enjoys life with her husband and three sons.

Jessie Blair is a gender-fluid person of Mohawk and Celtic descent. They are in their third year of an undergraduate degree studying sociology and creative writing at the University of British Columbia. They have published several articles, including interviews, in *Western Living* and *Vancouver* magazines. One article about an LGBTQI storyteller project was published in *Peace Arch News*. Some of their short fiction stories have appeared in various anthologies created by Filidh Publishing. Their focus is fiction and non-fiction stories. In their spare time they play the ukulele and sing off-key to their cat.

Simone Blais is a recovering journalist who writes in a communications department by day, edits works of non-fiction at night and escapes the clock by crafting fiction and poetry in between. Her poems have appeared in *Trickhouse* and *Other:____ Magazine*. An alumna of Simon Fraser University and Banff Centre for Arts and Creativity, she calls the Okanagan home and can be found online at simoneblais.com.

Sonja Boon is an award-winning writer, researcher and teacher. Her creative non-fiction has appeared in *Geist*, *The Ethnic Aisle* and donttalktomeaboutlove.org, and is forthcoming in two edited collections. In 2018 she received the Marina Nemat Award for Creative Writing from the University of Toronto School of Continuing Studies. Her critical memoir, titled *What the Oceans Remember: Searching for Belonging and Home*, was published in September 2019 by Wilfrid Laurier University Press.

Layla Cameron is a PhD candidate in the School of Communication at Simon Fraser University. Her research interests include celebrity culture and social media, and the representation on non-normative bodies in reality television and alternative media as seen through an intersectional feminist lens grounded in fat studies, gender studies, disability studies and critical race studies. Layla also works as a journalist, fat activist and documentary filmmaker. You can read more about Layla and her work at laylacameron.com.

Elizabeth Cook is an aspiring author who lives in a suburb of Toronto with her spouse and two children, Sully and Fitz, but will continue to call the Big Land, Labrador, her home. She believes sunrise is the best time of day and popcorn is a legitimate meal.

Andrea Hansell studied creative writing at Princeton University and earned a PhD in clinical psychology from the University of Michigan. She was a practising psychotherapist for many years and is now a consultant and scriptwriter for Glowmedia mental health education films. Her essays and short stories have appeared in publications including *Lilith*, *Intima*, *daCunha* and the *Lascaux Review*.

Jo Jefferson is a Toronto-based queer writer and parent who grew up in Nova Scotia. Their essay, "How I (Finally) Became a Genderqueer Parent," was included in Caitlin Press's anthology *Swelling with Pride*. Their first novel, *Lightning and Blackberries*, was released by Nimbus Publishing in 2008. When they're not writing or swimming, Jo hangs out with their kids, works at a community centre, explores the world and facilitates workshops with creators of all ages.

Heather M. Jones lives in Toronto with her husband, two young sons and two indignant cats. She can usually be found arguing with strangers on the internet or watching just one more episode on Netflix. You can follow Heather on Twitter and Instagram at @hmjoneswriter and on Facebook at /hmjoneswriter. To see more of her work, please visit hmjoneswriter.com.

Lynne Jones is a teacher and life coach specializing in self-acceptance and self-esteem issues. She is currently working on her first non-fiction book, exploring these subjects in an attempt to encourage more people to understand themselves and discover their true passion. In her spare time, she can be found chasing her naughty border collie across the Welsh mountains or rocking out with her band on a tiny electric ukulele in the South Wales Valleys.

Tara Mandarano is a Pushcart Prize–nominated writer and editor based in Canada. Her work has been featured on the front page of the *Huffington Post* and has also appeared in *Reader's Digest, Chatelaine, Today's Parent* and *Canadian Living*. She is also a chronic illness and mental health advocate. Please visit taramandarano.com to see more of her writing, or follow her on Instagram and Twitter at @taramandarano.

Tracy Manrell was assigned female at birth. They now identify as non-binary transmasculine and use they/them/he/him pronouns. Tracy has lived their life large in many ways through decades of being hounded internally and externally by size bias, fat stigma and gender dysphoria. Their life is full of complexities and love. They live on unceded territories of the Squamish, Tsleil-Waututh and Musqueam peoples with their beloved queer partner of nearly twenty-five years and their two funny, smart and kind teenagers. Tracy is one of the few folks in the world who has a full beard and whose kids call them Mama. It's a name of love, commitment and connection, not gender. In their spare time at home and afar, Tracy can almost always be found geocaching.

Caroline Many is a prairie nomad living in Metro Vancouver. She's been obsessed with online culture since the mid-1990s, when she first surfed the web as a staff music writer for EverythingCool.com. Over the past twenty years, her poetry, arts reviews and travel features have been published online and in print.

Jennifer Pownall served as the literary artist-in-residence for the City of Port Coquitlam. She co-facilitates a writers' group, is the blog content manager and editor for Joanne Fedler Media and works as an editor and contributing writer for *What's On! Port Coquitlam*. The *Globe and Mail* published her personal essay "I Am Bairnlorn," which speaks to her experiences with infertility, a topic she is exploring in detail as she composes her memoir, *Re:Birth*.

Sally Quon is a writer and photographer living in the beautiful Okanagan Valley, where she writes a weekly nature blog. When not out enjoying the back roads of the valley, she likes to spend time writing poetry and practising the art of quiet sitting. Her photography has appeared in *Canadian Geographic* magazine and in Nature Alberta's birding brochures. Her poetic musings have found homes in an assortment of places.

Rabbit Richards is learning how to exist on stolen land in a marginalized body. The Brooklyn-born poet writes into the awkward to explore the connections we deny and mischaracterize, blending the politics of race, love and gender with the emotional grounding of lived experience. They serve as the chairperson of the Anti-Oppression Committee for the board of Spoken Word Canada and as accessibility coordinator for Verses Festival of Words. When not touring, they make their home in Lek'leki, Downtown Eastside Vancouver.

Cate Root is a writer. She is part of the team behind Dogfish, a mixed-genre literary salon, and is building a better world with the New Orleans chapter of the Democratic Socialists of America. She writes love letters, poems, stories, essays, jokes, spells and way too many tweets. Find out more at cateroot.online.

Amanda (Ama) Scriver is a freelance journalist best known for being fat, loud and shouty on the internet. Her written work has appeared on *Healthline*, *BuzzFeed*, the *Washington Post*, FLARE, *The Walrus*, *Allure* and *Playboy*, among others. She finds joy in drag, reality television, bold lipstick and potato chips—in no particular order. You can follow her everywhere on the internet at @amascriver.

Cassie Stocks, in 2013, became the first woman in seventeen years to be awarded the Leacock Medal for humour writing for her novel *Dance, Gladys, Dance*. She has been published in magazines and journals such as *Avenue*, *Literary Mama*, *Other Voices* and *Reader's Digest*. Cassie lives in Eston, Saskatchewan, and is the town librarian.

Heather van Mil is a Canadian plus-sized body positivity advocate and freelance writer. She empowers women to love themselves and each other at every size. Her mission is to bring big, beautiful bodies to the mainstream, inspiring them to show up and take up space without apology. While her heart is split between the East and West Coasts, she currently resides in Halifax with her husband, two daughters and three fur babies. Follow her at @HeatherVanMil1.

Katy Weicker resides in Victoria, BC, and attends the University of Victoria, where she is chipping away at her BA in writing. A former staff writer for Camosun College's *Nexus Newspaper*, she has also had work appear in *Island Writer Magazine* as well as UVic's *The Warren* and *The Martlet*. She is pleased to report her cats have not attempted to eat her face to date—knock on wood!